Lampmaking

Lampmaking

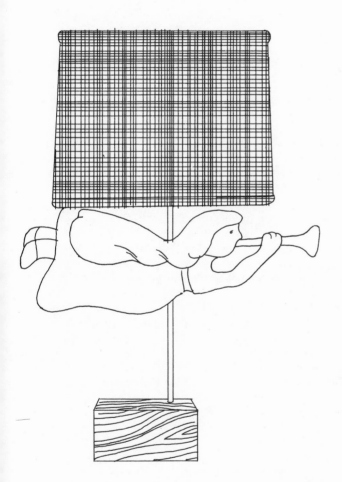

BRUCE W. MURPHY

& ANA G. LOPO

Sterling Publishing Co., Inc. New York

Oak Tree Press Co., Ltd London & Sydney

Dedicated to

Marie Di Gioia
Dick Ziff
David Burks

Published in 1980 by
Sterling Publishing Co., Inc.
Two Park Avenue
New York, N.Y. 10016

Distributed in Australia by Oak Tree Press Co., Ltd.,
P.O. Box J34, Brickfield Hill, Sydney 2000, N.S.W.

Library of Congress Cataloging in Publication Data

Murphy, Bruce W.
    Lampmaking: the ancient craft of making lamps.

    Bibliography

    1. Lamps. I. Lopo, Ana G., joint author. II. Title.
TT897.2.M87   745.59'3   76-16360
ISBN   0-8069-8462-7
Previously
ISBN 0-8473-1253-4
Oak Tree ISBN: 7061-2736-6

Printed in the United States of America

Acknowledgements

We'd like to express our most sincere appreciation to Marie Di Gioia, our talented and dear friend who encouraged us to write this book; to Dick Ziff who for years had many kind words about our craft projects; to Dr. David Burks for his invaluable assistance as a historian and a friend.

Many thanks to our parents who always had a good word for us, and especially our father, Segundo Lopo for sharing his photographic knowledge with us.

A very special thanks to all the museums and galleries who made it possible to obtain photographs and descriptions of their displays; to Frank and Loring McMillan, and all the helpful volunteers of the Richmondtown Restoration of Staten Island for their co-operation in letting us photograph their lighting devices; to Arnold Jacobs of the Brooklyn Museum; to Mrs. Alexandrina of the Museum of the American Indian; to Patricia Kelly of Mystic Seaport; to Isabel Silverman of the Cooper-Hewitt Museum; to Jo Sherman of the Metropolitan Museum of Art; Mrs. Fisher of Aladdin Galleries and Susan Teas of Lee Wards.

And, for their editorial assistance and guidance, our most sincere thanks to Maria Pallais and Walton Green.

Contents

LAMPMAKING

PART ONE

Section I

A Brief History

of Lampmaking

PART ONE

Section I

A BRIEF HISTORY

OF LAMPMAKING

Artificial light was probably born shortly after man discovered he could control fire, in prehistoric times. By using burning branches, placing some animal fat in a shell, hollow stone or animal skull, and adding moss to act as a floating wick, he had a fire that burned steadily for hours. With his portable light he could reach the deepest recesses of a cave and create cave paintings or perhaps conduct rituals. (Figure 1)

Stone and clay lamps have been found at archaeological digs in Egypt, Babylon, Palestine and other ancient locations. (Figure 2) These types of lamps have been used for 6,000 years and their design (Figures 3 and 4) varies from area to area, but basically remains the same -- grease to burn, and a wick for the light.

Some Egyptologists have given the Egyptians credit for inventing lamps. Lamps from the Old Kingdom were made of clay or stone. Torches and pieces of grease on a stick were also used as artificial light. (Figure 5)

The first pottery lamps are believed to have come from Egypt, and beautiful alabaster lamps were found among the treasures of King Tutankhamen, dating back to the 18th Dynasty (1580-1350 B. C.). (Figure 6)

Torches and floor lamps, more ornamental in design served to light temples for hundreds of years. And, ancient and Medieval lighting methods included fire baskets made of iron as well as torches and float lamps. (Figure 7)

In North America, the use of artificial light among most Indians was confined to torches and camp fires. For a long lasting flame, wood was fed into the fire periodically and did the job of illuminating well.

Torches were usually primitive -- rolled cane, pine knots and other flammable materials.

The Eskimos have had lamps for hundreds of years -- they were the only indigenous group who had this type of lighting devices in the Western hemisphere. Lamps varied in shape and design according to location. In the tundra they were clay or stone saucers; further north they favored soapstone with wide wick edges.

Some experts have indicated that groups in higher altitudes (having longer nights), favored longer lamp margins (where the moss wick was placed), for more lasting light.

The Eskimo lamp is made of stone and considered to be unique -- it is the only Eskimo lamp to have a carved human face on its underside. (Figures 8 and 9) The face can't be seen when the lamp is in use, and there are many theories about the purpose of the carving. Some propose that it was made to steady the lamp, others say it was simply a creative whim of its maker.

On the north west coast of the continent, several native groups burned fish bodies (candle fish) for light. Fish were abundant along the coast, and Northwest Indians were expert fishermen.

Another group of native Americans, the Apaches, used a cactus plant -- the Saguaro -- as a torch for lighting the way. And, some groups had beautifully decorated pottery vessels which they used for lamps. (Figure 10)

The Iroquois, of the League of Six Nations in the Northeast, had a law which required a messenger to carry a torch when nearing a village to show he was a friend.

American colonists were among the most imaginative people contributing to the history of artificial light. The hearth was the center of family life for early settlers, giving enough light for needlework and reading, and providing the right atmosphere for family unity.

In addition, "splint lights," thin slivers of wood loaded with resin, were also used by colonists, who appropriately called them "candle wood." Strips 8 inches to 10 inches in length were cut and carried about for portable lighting or placed in splint holders made of iron. (Figure 11)

"Rushlights" are considered to be an early relative of the candle. They are meadow rushes dipped in fats or tallow and used as candle-like lighting devices. They were placed on splint or rushlight holders made of wrought iron. A rush approximately two inches in length would burn for about an hour. (Fig. No. 12) The rushlight holder held the rushlight at an angle for burning.

Some experts however, claim that there's no evidence rughlight holders were used in the continent, but that rushes were carried about for light.

"Pan Lamps" are very shallow containers with the wick resting on the bottom of the pan. These simplest of all lamps, with no lip for resting a wick, are similar to those of the pre-historic cave man, and have also been used in different countries through the centuries.

The Crusies, not common in America, are open, made of one piece of wrought iron, and have an attachment for hanging. They have a curved bottom, making it impossible to rest them on a table or chair. There are some Crusies which have legs for standing, but these are considered very rare. They burn fish-oil, grease, and have a wick; they were used in Europe (in the north) Scotland, and Ireland. Crusies have a channel for the wick. (Fig. 13)

A double crusie, which has a similarly shaped drip pan underneath, is called a "Phoebe." (Fig. 14)

Many experts find the Betty, a better lamp, similar in design and shape to the ancient Roman and Greek lamps -- the body is one piece with a spout for the wick to rest and a high curved handle. (Figs. 15 & 16)

The iron Betty is usually cast or wrought iron in one solid piece and has a spindle to hang the lamp or to secure it between the stones of the fireplace. Bettys are covered, an improvement on the open Crusies, have a flat bottom with flaring sides, and a wick support not touching the sides.

Although Bettys varied in design throughout the years one problem remained -- the open wick was the source of smoke, and crust formed over it making the constant use of a pick necessary to keep the wick working.

There's some controversy to this day about the origin of the name "Betty." Most claim it derives from the old English word "bete" which means to make better -- a better lighting device. This lamp, in effect, was better than the open, shallow Crusies; Bettys were covered with lids

that opened on hinges or slid, and a wick support kept the wick slanted, two factors that made them better lamps.

Candles -- a wick and several coatings of fat -- date back to approximately the Eleventh Century, although candle-like devices existed in the First Century A. D. Some descriptions of these are "burning ropes," "ropes covered with wax," and "pillars of wax."

However, candles as we know them cannot be included among these. The candles we are familiar with, were used approximately 1,000 years ago.

Two methods were used in making candles: dipping and molding. Dipping, as the name implies, consisted of dipping a wick in hot tallow several times and then cooling the candle. For the molding method, candle molds were required and the candle substance was poured into the molds where a wick had been placed, and then cooled. (Fig. 17)

Beeswax was used in the Western world for church candles and for the wealthy. Less privileged classes used tallow candles. These were popular from the Middle Ages to the Nine-teenth Century. (Fig. 18)

Candle dipping was the monotonous task of the Seventeenth and Eighteenth Century housewives of Colonial America. This operation, usually done in the fall, was time consuming and directions had to be followed very carefully. With much luck and little help, the housewife managed to make a supply to last her for a while.

The lack of domestic animals in early Colonial times, prompted the settlers to use rush-lights, splint lights, torches and other means of lighting, until animals were more abundant and their tallow or fat could be used for candles.

Bayberry candles were valued by resourceful colonists as fragrant additions to the tallow and wax candles. These were made from the waxy substance of the fruit, which floated to the sur-face when boiled. They gave an exquisite fra-grance as they burned, and gave off no smoke. (Fig. 19)

Spermaceti candles were the most luxurious of all, and were made from the substance obtained from the head of the sperm whale. These candles were more translucent and gave twice as much light as the tallow candles. The process of obtaining spermaceti was introduced around 1750.

Candle molds no doubt, simplified candle making, but dipping was a cheaper process. Very early molds date back to the Fourteenth Century.

Decorative wrought iron pieces were used by wealthy families to hold candles. Also used were silver, wood, tin, brass, pewter, and others. Pierced lanterns, wall sconces, and chandeliers were also used. (Figs. No. 20 & 21) The variety of candle holders and carriers is tremendous.

The iron candlestick was usually made as a cylinder and a base. Some have a sliding lever in the cylinder to push the candle up as it burned; these are reputed to date back to the Eighteenth Century. (Figs. 22 & 23)

"Pricket" candlesticks usually have an iron base with a spike to stick the candle. (Fig. 24)

Some spring candlesticks used from the latter part of 1600 to about 1845, force the candle up by a spring as it burns, eliminating drippins. Others were highly decorative silver gilt. (Fig. 25)

The Shakers, a religious group well-known for their fine craftsmanship and inventive designs, had a movable wall sconce which they could adjust to several levels. (Fig. 26)

Candlestands, made of wrought iron or wood, were also used to hold candles and are still admired for their graceful designs. (Fig. 27)

The whale-oil lamp is an American invention -- at least the burner is -- which some attribute to Benjamin Franklin. In 1787 the upright wick tube and closed-in front (to avoid spills), were introduced by John Miles. The American whale-oil lamp is a descendant of these lighting improvements. (Fig. 28)

One expert's easy way of identifying a whale-oil lamp burner is to look for a burner that fits and screws into the reservoir, has at least one round wick tube and has slots used for wick adjusting. Very rarely can one find whale-oil lamps with a globe for protecting the flame.

Whale-oil lamps are made of glass and pewter, and the fluid used as an illuminant was the oil processed from the blubber of the whale and sperm oil, from the head of the sperm whale. (Fig. 29)

One interesting type of whale-oil lamp is the "Peg" lamp. These have pegs which can be inserted into candlesticks. (Fig. 30)

Economy -- not wanting to discard brass and silver candle holders -- is believed to be the cause for this interesting design.

Argand burners, invented by Ami Argand a Swiss chemist, consist of a circular wick placed in a hollow cylinder allowing for the passage of air. This type of burner improved lighting tremendously.

Kerosene (refined from petroleum), cost less than other illuminants and gave an excellent light. A flat wick burner and turnip-shaped reservoir which allows a glass lamp chimney to be attached, created a new need for production of glass lamps. These lamps became popular in the second half of the Nineteenth Century. (Figs. 31, 32, 33, 34)

Gas lamps, important when gas lighting began to be piped into American homes from a central supply of gas late in the Nineteenth Century, are colorfully designed. These lamps and bright mantels, did much to aid the cause of gas lighting in the 1890s.

Beautiful table lamps, outdoor lanterns, wall brackets and gaseliers from that era are very decorative. Victorian desire for colored glass patterns are reflected on the design of these lighting pieces.

Electricity was supplied to the public by 1882. In the early 1900s the Art Nouveau movement inspired the blown glass light shades. These lasted until the 1930s. (Fig. 35)

Louis C. Tiffany, Steuben Glass Works and other famous glass specialists made signed shades which are highly priced collector's items today. (Fig. 36)

Tiffany was well-known for his shades of iridescent glass in the form of flowers and leaves.

Then came a curious turnabout: The American Arts and Crafts Movement and a return to simple, handicrafted and functional designs for furnishings, including lamps.

Many of the lamps we have explored in this brief history, are the result or the cause of social changes, culture and a positive reflection of man's ingenuity in the area of illumination.

PART ONE

Section II

Photos and

Illustrations

PART ONE

Section II

PHOTOS
AND ILLUSTRATIONS

Figure 1. Prehistoric Float Lamp -- made of stone and uses moss for the wick. Some lamps of this type are 20,000 years old.

Figure 2. Ancient Lamp -- Palestine. (Courtesy of Aladdin Galleries, *New York, N. Y.*)

Figure 3. Ancient Near East-Ceramics-Pottery. Palestinian, I Millenium B. C. (1000-586). Tell-duweir, Palestine. Lamp of red earthenware, unglazed. (The Metropolitan Museum of Art, gift of Harris D. & H. Dunscombe Colt, 1934.)

Figure 4. Ancient Near East Lamp. Palestinian, I Millenium. Tell-duweir, Palestine. Buff earthenware, unglazed. (The Metropolitan Museum of Art, gift of Harris D. and H. Dunscombe Colt, 1934.)

Figure 5. A Glazed Terra-cotta Night Light representing the head and arm of a woman wearing a broad necklace. Egypt, early Roman period. (Courtesy of the Brooklyn Museum, Charles Edwin Wilbour Foundation.)

Figure 6. Lamp for Four Lights, Bronze. Mingles Coptic and Islamic details, the handle represents a fantastic animal. 9 A. D. (Courtesy of the Brooklyn Museum, Charles Edwin Wilbour Foundation.)

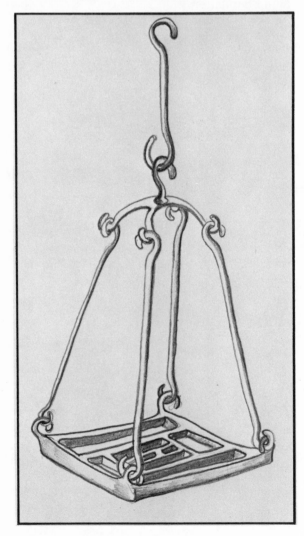

Figure 7. Fire Basket -- Ancient and Medieval periods. Burns wood and fats.

Figure 8. Eskimo Lamp -- (side view) stone. (Courtesy of the Museum of the American Indian, Heye Foundation.)

Figure 9. Eskimo Lamp -- with base representing a man's head. Alaska (14 3/8 " long, weight 27½ pounds). (Courtesy of the Museum of the American Indian, Heye Foundation.)

Figure 10. Early Lamp Shaped Pottery Vessels, with painted decoration. Center: 5" diameter. Socorro County, New Mexico. (Courtesy of the Museum of the American Indian, Heye Foundation.)

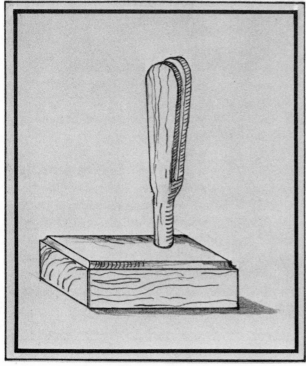

Figure 11. Splint Light -- thin slivers of wood were dipped in resin for longer lasting light.

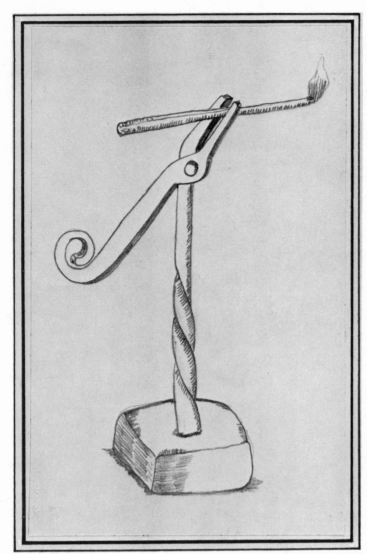

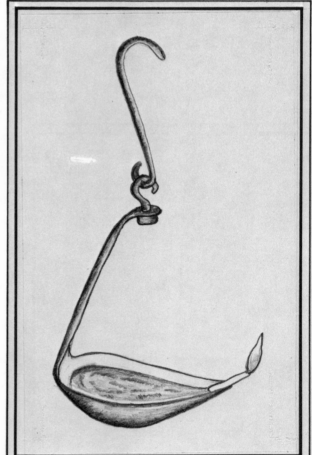

Figure 12. Rushlight Holder -- used for holding rushlights at an angle for burning. Usually made of hand wrought iron.

Figure 13. Crusie Lamp -- a shallow, grease lam with wick.

Figure 14. Double Crusie or "Phoebe" Lamp.
(Authors' collection)

Figure 15. Betty Lamp -- made of brass with a copper bottom. It has an iron wick support, iron handle, iron hook and a brass chain. The object is marked "P. D. 1858" and was made by Peter Derr. (Courtesy of Mystic Seaport, Mystic, Ct.)

Figure 16. Ancient Lamp in the Roman and Greek style. Compare to Betty Lamp for similarities.

Figure 17. Candle Mold for Six Candles -- made of tin. This one is from the kitchen of the Lake-Tysen House, (c. 1740). Candle holder with candle lift. Richmond Restoration. (Courtesy of the Staten Island Historical Society.)

Figure 18. Adjustable, Floor Candlestand -- at the oldest elementary school in the United States (c. 1696) Voorlezer's House, Richmond Restoration. (Courtesy of the Staten Island Historical Society.)

Figure 19. Brass Candlestick with a Lift, and Candle Snuffers -- a scissors-like accessory used to catch the candle wick after it was cut. (Courtesy of the Staten Island Historical Society.)

Figure 20. Wrought Iron Candle Holder. French
(c. 1750) (Courtesy of the Cooper Hewitt Museum, The Smithsonian Institution, New York, New
York.)

Figure 21. Porcelain Candlesticks -- Chinese ex-
port, porcelain, Chieng Lung (1736 - 1795).
(Courtesy of the Brooklyn Museum, gift of Donald S. Morrison.)

Figure 22. Iron Spring Candle Holder (Courtesy of the Cooper Hewitt Museum, the Smithsonian Institution, New York, NY.)

Figure 23. Birdcage Candle Holder with Candle Lift, (wood). Vertical bars probably for protection of the flame. Some experts think the bars were just for decoration. Also in the photo, a wooden rushlight holder with socket for candle. These were found at the carpenter shop (c. 1830) at the Richmond Restoration. (Courtesy of the Staten Island Historical Society.)

Figure 24. Pricket Candle Holder. This is one of the oldest forms of candle holders. Used by the nobility and the church.

Figure 25. Silver Gilt Wall Sconce. England (1665-66). (Courtesy of the Brooklyn Museum, gift of Donald S. Morrison.)

Figure 26. Shaker Adjustable Candle Sconce. Made of wood.

Figure 28. Pewter whale-oil Lamp. 5 ½ " high, 3 ¾ " diameter of base. (Courtesy of Mystic Seaport, Mystic, Ct.)

Figure 27. Double, Adjustable Floor Candlestand. Voorlezer's House. (Courtesy of the Staten Island Historical Society.)

Figure 29. Glass Lamp, fluid burning. Lake-Tysen House, Richmondtown Restoration. (Courtesy of the Staten Island Historical Society.)

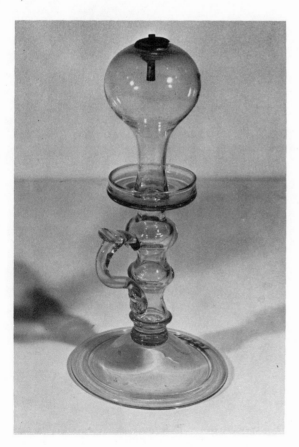

Figure 30. This glass-blown lamp is a peg lamp in a candlestick. It is 6 ¼ " high with a base 4 ¼ " in diameter. (Courtesy of Mystic Seaport, Mystic Ct.)

Figure 31. Shelves containing matches, lamp parts, and candles are a typical example of an 1850's general store. Stephen's Store, Richmondtown Restoration. (Courtesy of the Staten Island Historical Society.)

Figure 33. Decorative Lamp with Marble Base. (c. 1837) Stephen's House, Richmondtown Restoration. (Courtesy of the Staten Island Historical Society.)

Figure 32. Lamp -- made in two-colors, the chimney is clear and the base yellow. Lake-Tysen House. (Courtesy of the Staten Island Historical Society.)

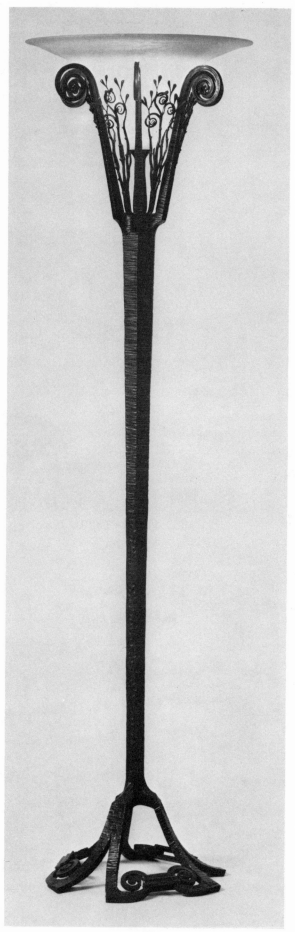

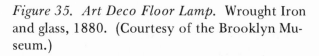

Figure 34. Kerosene Lamp -- Stephen's Store
(Courtesy of the Staten Island Historical Society.)

Figure 35. Art Deco Floor Lamp. Wrought Iron
and glass, 1880. (Courtesy of the Brooklyn Museum.)

Figure 36. Tiffany Lamp. Dragonfly design
(1900 - 1920). (Courtesy of the Brooklyn
Museum. Gift of Laura L. Barnes.)

Figure 37. Pierced Tin Lantern. With a candle
inside throws a beautiful, soft light. Also used
with whale-oil lamp inside. (Courtesy of the Stat-
en Island Historical Society.)

Figure 38. An unusual lamp found at a carpenter's shop -- it has an arm extension. Richmondtown Restoration. (Courtesy of the Staten Island Historical Society.)

Figure 39. Burning Fluid Lamp. Lake-Tysen lamp (Courtesy of the Staten Island Historical Society.)

Figure 41. Lantern (glass and tin), protecting the flame of a whale-oil burner.

Figure 40. Carriage Lamp, fluid-burning with reflectors. (Courtesy of Staten Island Historical Society.)

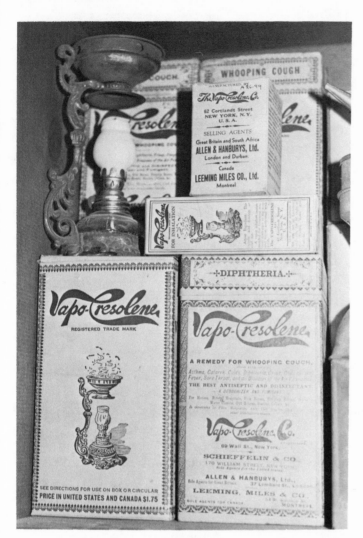

Figure 42. Vaporizer Lamp -- We came across this example of a Vapo-Cresolene lamp. The medication was placed on the dish above the flame of the burning fluid lamp. The patient suffering from asthma, whooping cough, diptheria would breathe the beneficial vapors to help his condition. Stephen's Store (Courtesy of Staten Island Historical Society.)

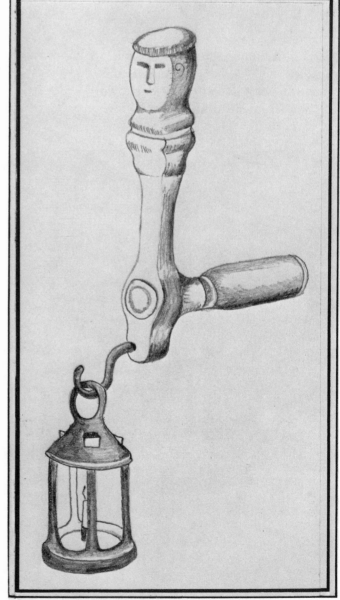

Figure 43. Lamplifter and Lantern, carried by officers when making the rounds on a ship at night.

Figure 44. N. G. FISH Ship's Chandlery -- Bow lights and side lights anchor, stern and masthead lights, in galvanized iron, brass and copper with plain glass, ruby and green globes ; lanterns of every variety and size were sold at the ship's chandlery. The massive rope coiled in the foreground, capstans and barrels for supplies were the most important marine supplies stocked in the chandlery, the ship's store. (Courtesy of Mystic Seaport, Mystic, Ct.)

PART TWO

Section I

Lampmaking Tools

PART TWO

Section I

LAMPMAKING
TOOLS

The following are a few of the tools that will be helpful to you in making the lamp projects presented in this book. All of the tools used are very inexpensive and can be bought at most hardware stores. Each tool is simple and easy to operate. Even a total novice will have no trouble using them. As you will see, lampmaking is not the complicated art you once thought it to be.

DREMEL MOTO - SHOP

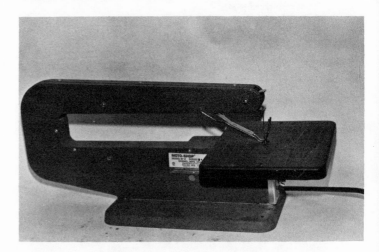

This electric scroll saw will make the sawing of the wooden lamp parts very easy. If you don't have a Dremel saw, a hand held coping saw will do.

ELECTRIC DRILL

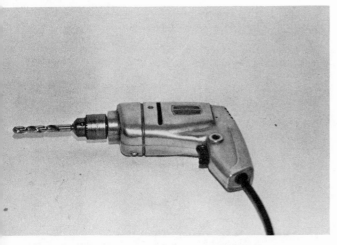

The electric drill is one tool that will be most helpful in the making of lamps.

PIPE CUTTER

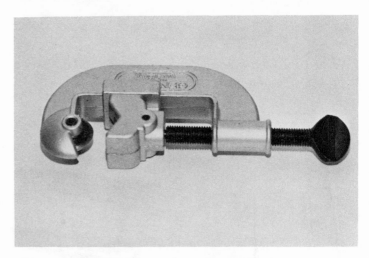

Pipe cutter is used to cut brass lamp pipe to required lengths.

TAP AND DIE WRENCH

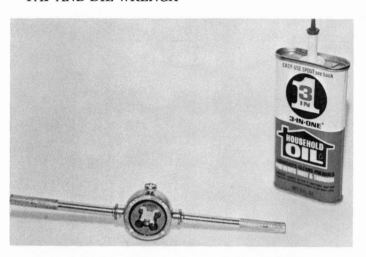

Tap and die wrench is used to thread lamp pipe. Machine oil is placed on the end of the pipe to make threading easier.

DOWELING JIG

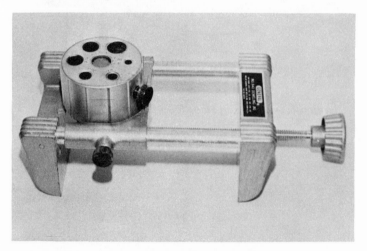

Doweling jig is used to guide an electric drill in the boring of a straight hole in wood bases.

HAND RIVET GUN AND RIVETS

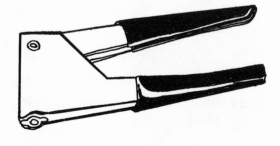

WIRE STRIPPER

Wire stripper makes the removal of wire insulation very easy.

CARBORUNDUM BIT

Drilling a Hole in Glass

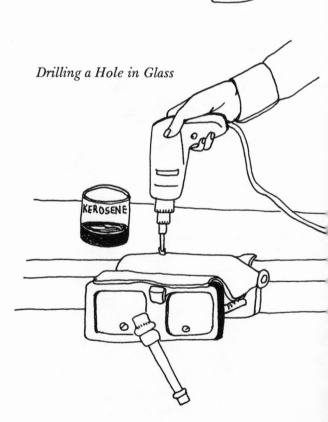

LAMP CORD STRIPPING AND WIRING

To prepare lamp wire for connection:

A) Split down the center with a sharp knife. Be careful not to cut through the wire insulation into the metal wires.

B) The ends of the wire insulation are removed with a wire stripper or sharp knife. It is best to remove at least an inch of the insulation.

C) The wire inside of the insulation is not a single wire, but several strands of wire. These must be twisted together to form a single wire.

D) To connect wires together, the simplest way is with a pigtail splice. This is made simply by twisting the two wires together.

E) Solderless connectors make this splice permanent and safe. To use, insert the spliced wires into the tip of the connector. Then twist the connector clockwise until it grips the wire securely on the inside.

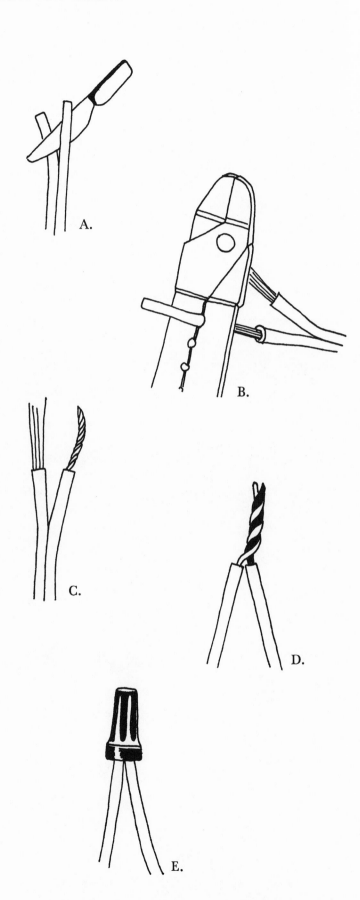

DIRECTIONS

How to Drill a Hole in Glass:

You will first need a carborundum bit, which is especially made for drilling glass. This bit, some kerosene, and a hand or electric drill are the only tools you will need. Drilling a hole in glass is an easy but slow process. First dip the bit into th kerosene and place a drop on the bottle where the hole is to be drilled. The kerosene will help reduce the friction caused by the drilling. Dip the bit into the kerosene frequently during the entire drilling process. The bottle can be held securely in a vise to make the drilling easier. Cover the bottle with a felt cloth to prevent it from being scratched by the vise jaws. If you apply too much pressure while drilling, you can cause the bottle to break. Do not try to drill the hole all at once as a great deal of heat from friction builds up while drilling. Allow the bit and the bottle time to cool off periodically while you are drilling.

PART TWO

Section II

Lamp Parts

PART TWO

Section II

LAMP PARTS

A.   B.   C.   D.

A. *Brass loop*
B. *Locktight washer*
C. *Arm end nozzle with side hole tapped*
D. *Knurled brass cap*

M.   N.   O.

M. *Lamp adaptor for candle sticks and bottle necks*
N. & O. *Spun brass bases*

E.   F.   G.   H.

E. *Hex locknut*
F. *Cord bushing inlet*
G. *Round locknut*
H. *Rubber washer*

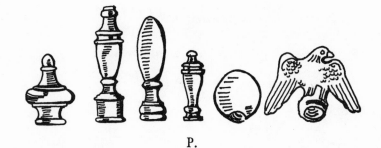

P.

P. *Turned brass finials*

I.   J.   K.   L.

I. *Shade rest bushing*
J. *Beaded nozzle*
K. *Reducing coupling*
L. *90° Angle nozzle*

Q.

Q. *Turned brass necks and spindles*

HARPS

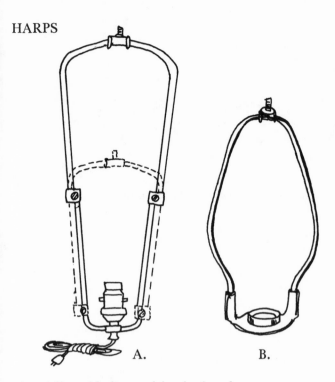

A.

B.

C.

D.

A.   Adjustable harp with wired socket

B. Swivel screw on harp, which screws onto socket

C. Two piece detachable harp and base

D.   Harp which converts washer-type shade to fit a bulb.

LAMP PIPE

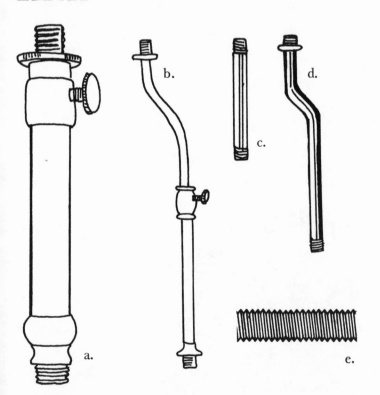

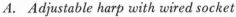

a.

b.

c.

d.

e.

THREADED NIPPLES

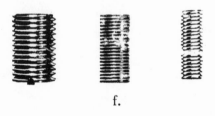

f.

a.   Adjustable lamp pipe

b.   Adjustable figurine extension lamp pipe

c.   Brass straight lamp pipe 1/8 I. P. threaded on both ends

d.   Brass plated bent figurine pipe

e.   1/8IP threaded lamp pipe

f.   Threaded nipples steel and brass
Standardized lamp pipe is referred to as 1/8 inch I.P. The pipe has an inner diameter of 1/8 " and an outer diameter (O. D.) of 3/8".

Solderless connectors

Clip on in-line
on-off switch

Brass
chimney
holder

Swag hook kit

Wired oil
lamp
converter

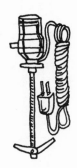

Bottle or
vase lamp
converter kit

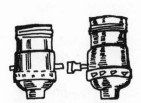

Lamp sockets:
push and 3-way

Fixture
chain

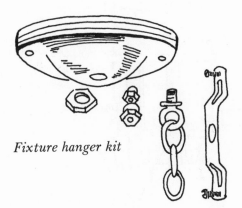

Fixture hanger kit

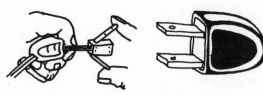

Clip on plug requires
no stripping of insulation

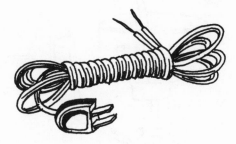

No. 18 Parallel lamp cord

LIGHT SOCKET ASSEMBLY

ELECTRIC CANDLE SOCKET ASSEMBLY

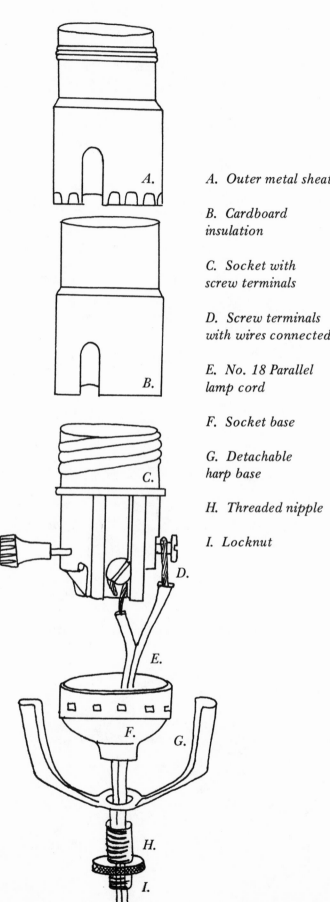

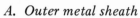

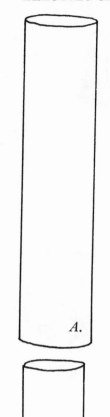

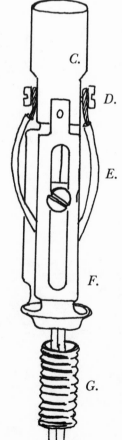

A. Outer metal sheath

B. Cardboard insulation

C. Socket with screw terminals

D. Screw terminals with wires connected

E. No. 18 Parallel lamp cord

F. Socket base

G. Detachable harp base

H. Threaded nipple

I. Locknut

A. Plastic candle sleeve

B. Cardboard insulator

C. Socket

D. Screw terminals

E. No. 18 Parallel lamp cord

F. Adjustable hickey

G. Threaded nipple

PART THREE

Section I

Lampshade Making

PART THREE

Section I

LAMPSHADE MAKING

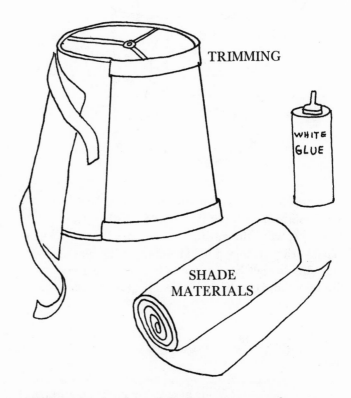

TRIMMING

WHITE GLUE

SHADE MATERIALS

This is the simplest of shade covers to make. You just glue a new shade cover over the old one. Dilute white glue with water, and brush it onto old shade cover. Carefully adhere new shade covering to the old. Press out all wrinkles and bubbles. Conceal all edges with a decorative trim. For a complete guide to shade making, obtain a copy of "Making Lampshades" by Angela Fishburn. (Drake Publishers, 1975)

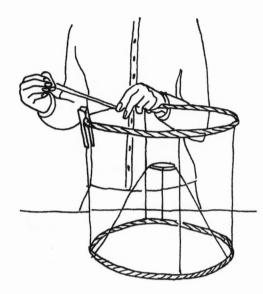

Carefully remove the old shade cover and use it as a pattern for your new shade. With cotton bias tape, wrap the entire frame. Hold tape in place with a clothes pin. The coils of the bias tape should tightly overlap each other. Fasten the two ends together with needle and thread.

Your new shade cover should overlap ½ " where the ends meet. The shade cover is then glued to the edges. Use clothes pins to hold cover in place while glue dries.

The top and bottom edges should be covered with a decorative trimming. Carefully glue the trimming to the shade edges, and wrap it far enough inside to cover the tape-bound wire frame.

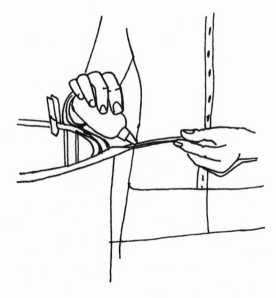

PART THREE

Section II

Lamp Projects

DUCK DECOY LAMP

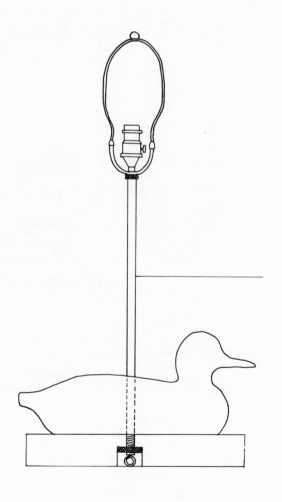

DUCK DECOY LAMP

Duck decoys are becoming very popular -- antique wooden ones with collectors, and even inexpensive contemporary versions, for their decorative qualities. They are easily available at antique shops, flea markets, and most sporting goods stores. A good mail order source for decoys is Herter's Inc. (See sources for address.) If you feel "adventurous" and want to carve your own decoy, the book "Wild Fowl Decoys" by Joel Barber, offers complete instructions for this type of project. A duck decoy lamp will make a beautiful lighting accessory for any room.

MATERIALS

Wooden decoy
Wooden base, pine ¾ ” x 8 ” x 13 ”
1/8 ” brass pushing inlet
Socket
Harp
8 ’ parallel lamp cord set
Locknuts
Felt pad
Shade of your choice
12 ” figurine bend lamp pipe
½ pint oil wood stain
White wood glue
Finial

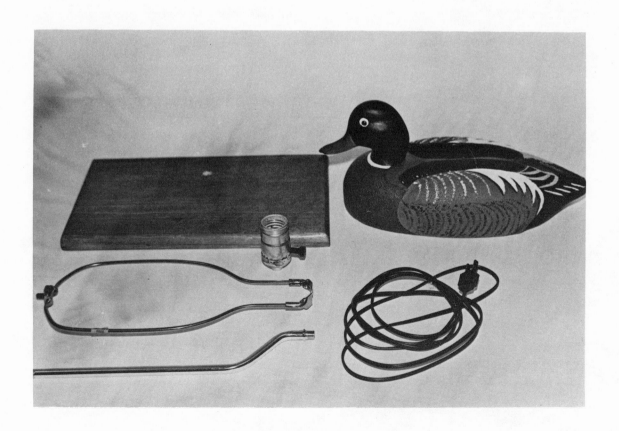

DIRECTIONS

STEP 1

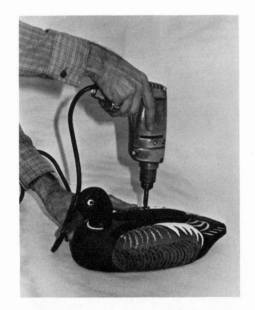

STEP 2

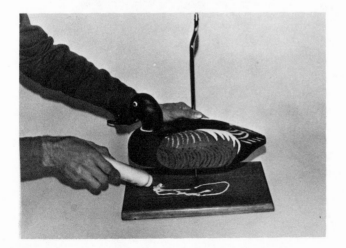

STEP 3

STEP 1 -- Cut wood for base, sand down all edges, and stain.

STEP 2 -- Drill 3/8 " hole through back, right side of the decoy and base. Follow diagram for exact positioning of holes.

STEP 3 -- Insert lamp pipe through decoy and connect to the base with locknuts. Glue decoy to the base with white wood glue.

STEP 4 -- Insert wire through bushing inlet and through lamp pipe. Connect the wires to socket.

STEP 5 -- Glue felt pad to base.

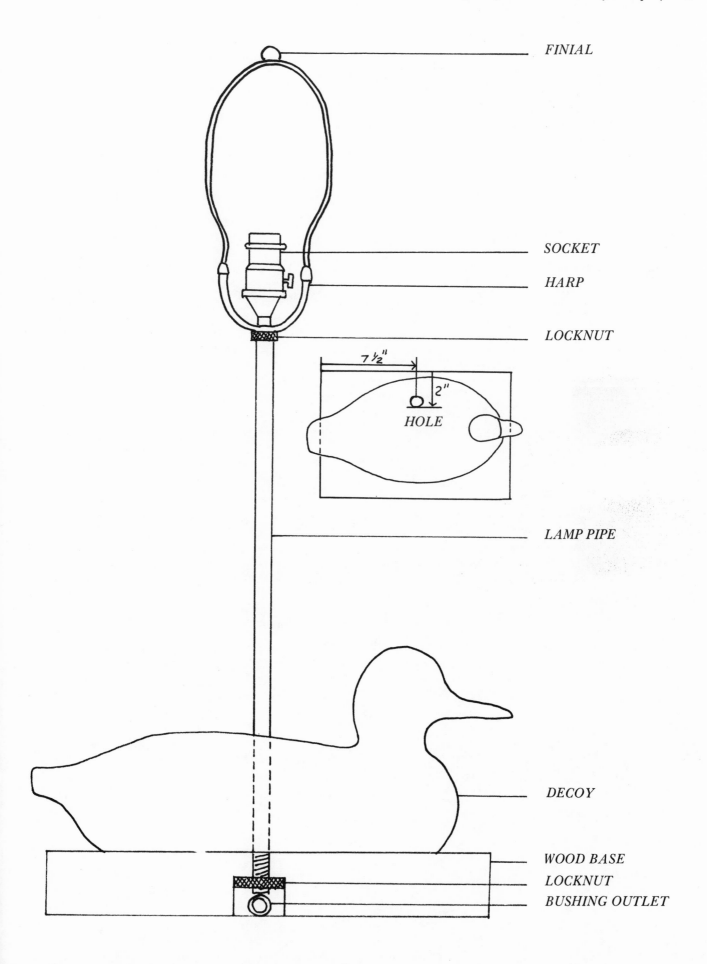

FINIAL

SOCKET

HARP

LOCKNUT

7 ½"

2"

HOLE

LAMP PIPE

DECOY

WOOD BASE

LOCKNUT

BUSHING OUTLET

SNIPE DECOY LAMP

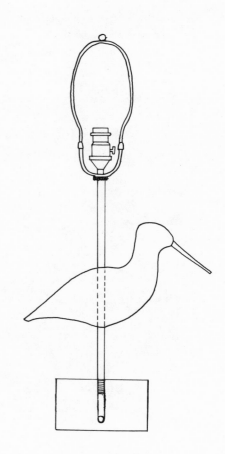

SNIPE DECOY LAMP

This snipe decoy lamp is an unusual and striking lamp project for anyone's home. The snipe, a marshbird relative of the sandpiper, has delicate contours and a graceful look about it. These qualities make the "Snipe Decoy Lamp" a unique addition to any room decor.

MATERIALS

Snipe decoy
Lamp pipe, straight, threaded both ends, 16 "
Wooden base, pine, 4 " x 4 " x 6 "
Locknut
Socket
Harp
Parallel lamp cord set 8 '
Felt pad
Shade of your choice
Finial

DIRECTIONS

STEP 1 Drill 3/8 " hole through decoy.

STEP 2 -- To give the pine base an antique look is quite easily achieved. Remove pieces of the top edges with a pocket knife. A small piece of chain can be used to beat on the wood to give it an aged appearance, and a wire brush will enable you to raise the grain on the wood. Next, lightly sand all rough edges smooth.

STEP 3 -- Paint base with an acrylic paint that matches or corresponds to the dominant color in the decoy. When the paint dries, take a piece of fine steel wool (available at supermarkets) and rub the paint until parts of the raw wood start to show through the paint.

STEP 4 -- With the aid of a doweling jig, drill holes in base for lamp pipe and cord inlet.

STEP 5 -- Insert pipe into the base and connect wire to socket. Glue felt pad to base.

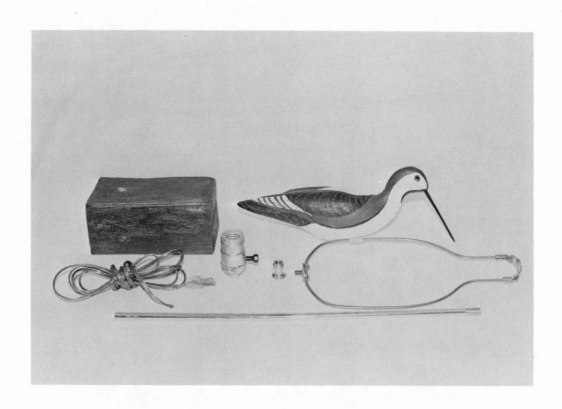

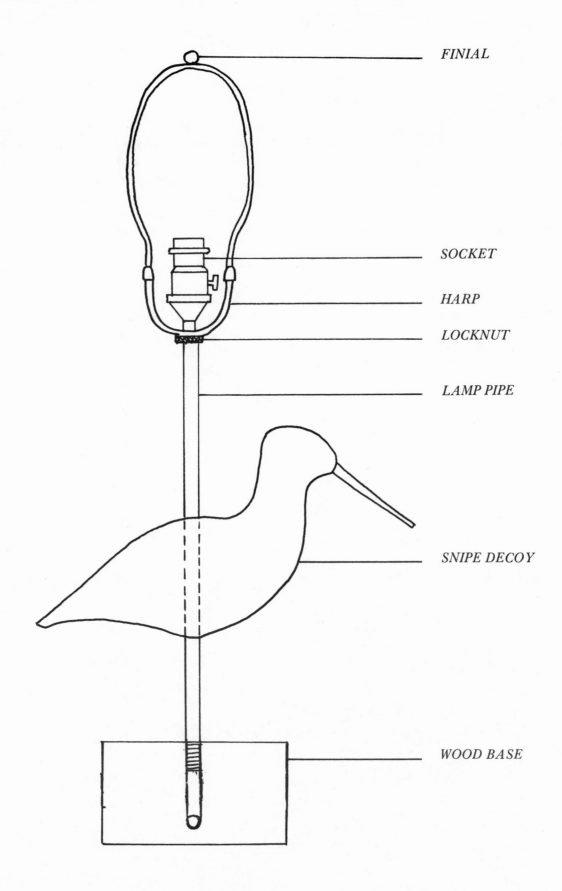

FINIAL

SOCKET

HARP

LOCKNUT

LAMP PIPE

SNIPE DECOY

WOOD BASE

ANTIQUE DOLL LAMP

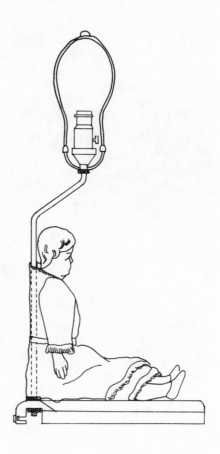

ANTIQUE DOLL LAMP

A child or teen-ager will enjoy this lamp as much as a doll collector. The doll can be an inexpensive replica or an original antique. Either way it will be safe, as the lamp tubing goes behind and under the doll's dress, avoiding any techniques that will disfigure or break the doll. You will find several stores that specialize in China, bisque, and wooden doll replicas listed under sources.

MATERIALS

Small doll of your choice
1 Figurine bend lamp pipe 11"
1 Socket
1 Harp
1 Cord 6' long
3 Locknuts
1 Wooden base ¾" x 8" x 8"
1 Felt base
1 Bushing, cord inlet
1 Shade of your choice
1 Finial

DIRECTIONS

STEP 1 -- Cut wooden base 8" x 8". Sand and stain.

STEP 2 -- Drill holes for pipe and cord outlet.

STEP 3 -- Insert pipe through the back of the doll's dress, and secure pipe to the base with two locknuts.

STEP 4 -- Insert wire through pipe and connect to electric socket.

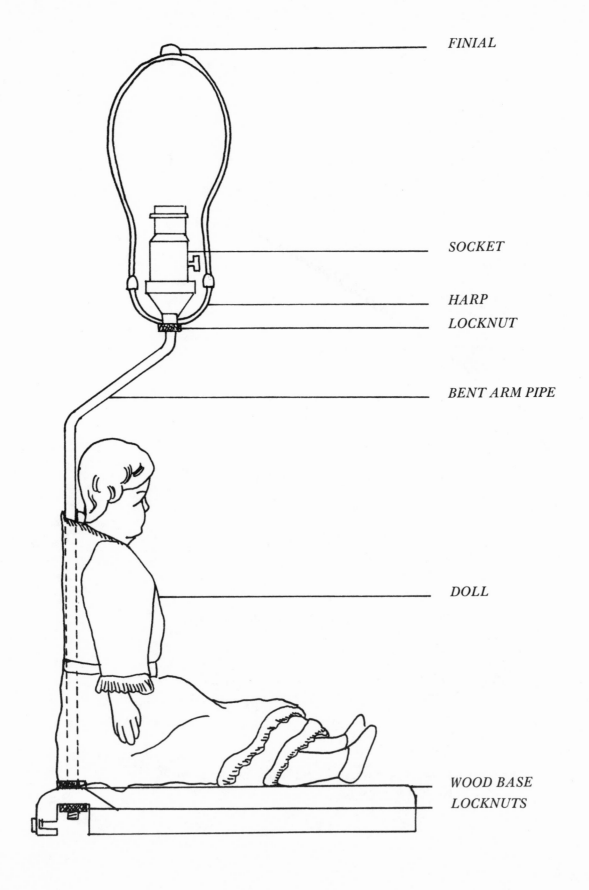

FINIAL

SOCKET

HARP

LOCKNUT

BENT ARM PIPE

DOLL

WOOD BASE

LOCKNUTS

WINE BOTTLE LAMP

WINE BOTTLE LAMP

Instead of throwing away that old wine bottle, why not turn it into that perfect lamp you've been looking for. It will go great in your bar, game room or studio.

MATERIALS

1 Wine bottle with reed covering
1 4" threaded nipple
1 Brass vase cap to fit bottle top
1 Neck
1 Sheet of cork to wrap around nipple
1 Socket
1 Harp
1 Parallel Lamp cord 8'
1 Locknut
1 3/8 ' glass drill bit
1 Shade of your choice

DIRECTIONS

STEP 1 -- With glass drill bit, bore 3/8 " opening in side of bottle.

STEP 2 -- Insert wire through hole and pull through the neck of the bottle. Place nipple over wire and connect brass cap and neck to nipple with locknuts.

STEP 3 -- Wrap enough cork around nipple to insure a tight fit in the bottle neck.

STEP 4 -- Connect wire to electric socket.

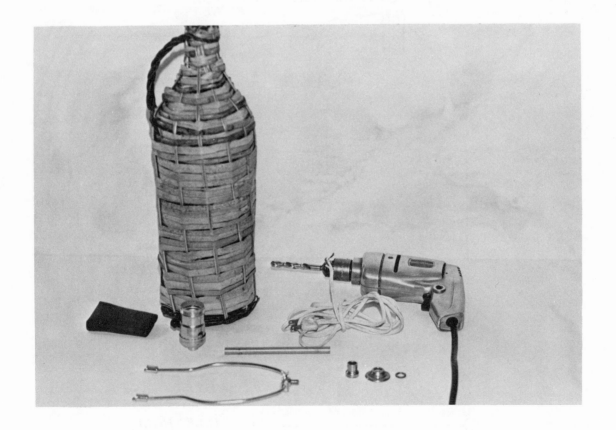

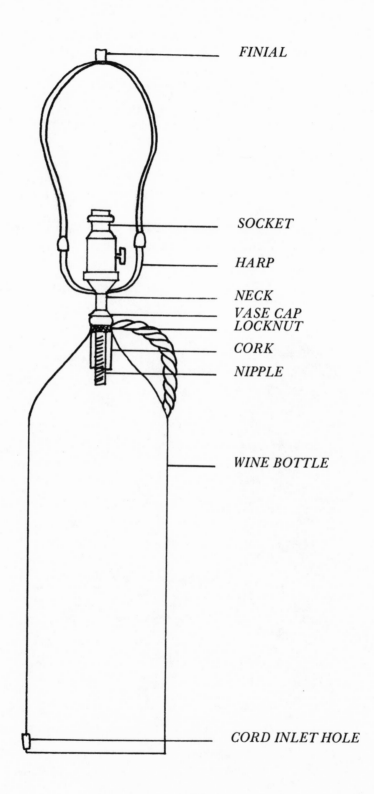

FINIAL

SOCKET

HARP

NECK
VASE CAP
LOCKNUT
CORK
NIPPLE

WINE BOTTLE

CORD INLET HOLE

ROPE LAMP

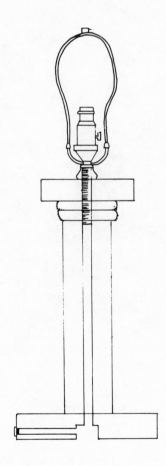

ROPE LAMP

One of the most important tools of the sailor was rope. Sailor's knots which had functional applications, became the basis for today's macrame, according to some experts. A nautical mood inspired this rope lamp, which is easily made by winding inexpensive rope around a rolling pin.

DIRECTIONS

It may be necessary to drill a hole through the entire length of your rolling pin if it does not come this way.

STEP 1 -- Drill 3/8" hole in center of the 3" and 5" wooden circles. Counterbore bottom to aid in inserting wire through bushing inlet.

STEP 2 -- Sand and stain the two wood circles.

STEP 3 -- Center holes in wooden top and base over the hole in rolling pin and glue together with wood glue.

STEP 4 -- Connect neck to base with 2" nipple and screw threaded nipple into rolling pin hole.

STEP 5 -- With upholsterer's tack secure one end of the rope to the top of rolling pin. Wrap rope securely around the entire rolling pin and secure at the bottom with a second tack.

STEP 6 -- Insert wire through bushing inlet and through center of rolling pin. Connect to socket.

MATERIALS

1 9" rolling pin
1 ¾" x 5" round wooden base
1 ¾" x 3" round wooden top
15" of 3/8" Manila rope
2 Upholsterer's tacks
1 1/8" bushing inlet
1 2" nipple
1 beaded neck
White wood glue
1 Socket
1 Harp
1 Parallel lamp cord 6'
1 Felt pad
1 Shade of your choice
1 Finial

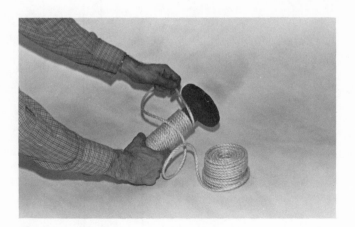

WINDING ROPE

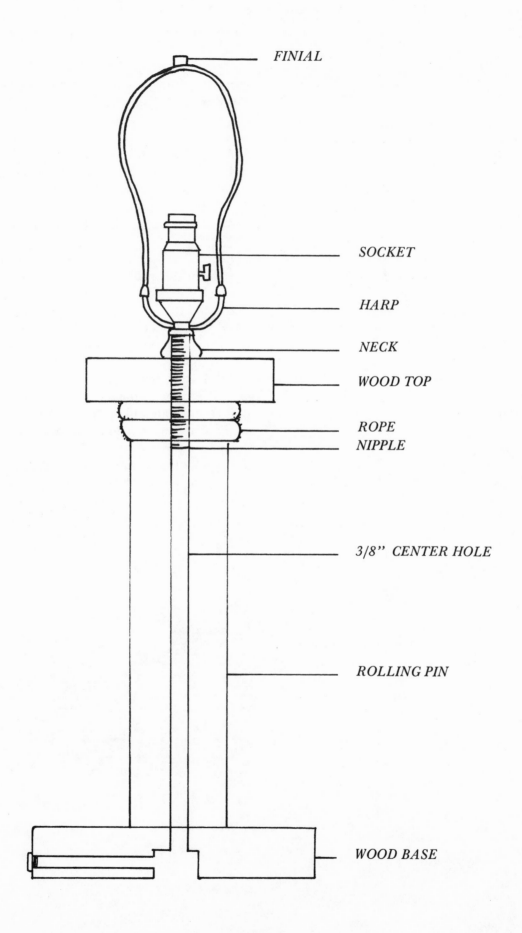

FINIAL

SOCKET

HARP

NECK

WOOD TOP

ROPE
NIPPLE

3/8" CENTER HOLE

ROLLING PIN

WOOD BASE

GINGER JAR LAMP

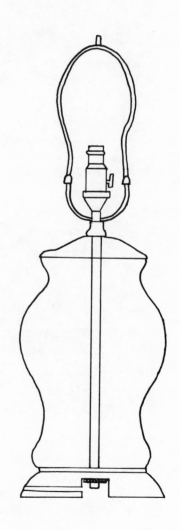

GINGER JAR LAMP

The shapely ginger jar, traditionally thought to be the container that brought spices from the Far East, has become very popular in the past few years. This ginger jar was bought at a dime store for only a few dollars. You can turn it into a most beautiful lamp for a fraction of what it would cost you at any store.

MATERIALS

1 Glass ginger jar available at variety stores
1 Round wood base
1 Brass vase cap to fit jar top
1 Straight lamp pipe, threaded both ends
1 Locknut
1 Neck
1 Socket
1 Harp
1 8' parallel lamp cord
1 3/8" glass drill bit
1 Felt pad
1 Shade of your choice
1 Finial

DIRECTIONS

STEP 1 -- You can either make your own wooden base or buy one to fit your jar base from one of the lamp supply houses listed under sources.

STEP 2 -- Follow directions previously given for drilling hole in glass, and drill 3/8" hole in bottom center of jar. Drill 3/8" hole also into center of wood base. Counterbore wood base for insertion of locknut. Drill horizontal hole for cord inlet.

STEP 3 -- Insert pipe through bottle and wood base. Secure to base with locknut.

STEP 4 -- Place brass cap over pipe and onto jar mouth. Secure to pipe with threaded neck.

STEP 5 -- Insert wire and connect to socket.

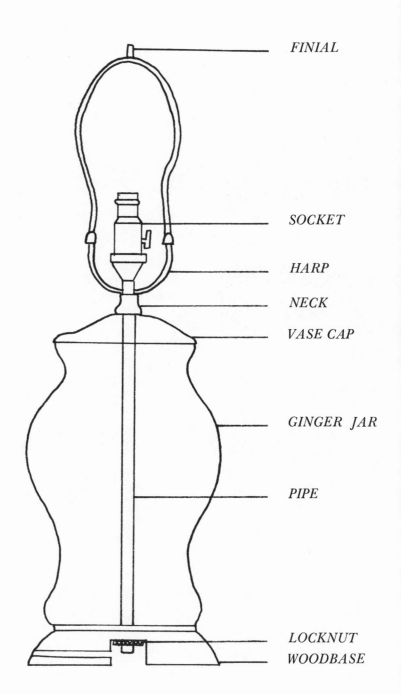

FINIAL

SOCKET

HARP

NECK

VASE CAP

GINGER JAR

PIPE

LOCKNUT

WOODBASE

ANGEL WEATHERVANE LAMP

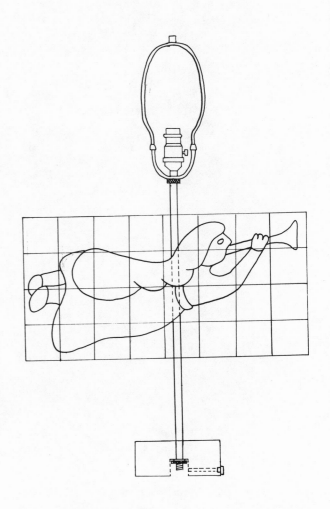

ANGEL WEATHERVANE LAMP

In Early American times, weathervanes were used on top of buildings, where they could be seen from far away. They could be called our first weathermen, since they provided weather information at a glance. An interesting aspect of weathervanes is the subjects people chose for them -- the farmer chose a horse or cow for the top of his barn; villages next to the sea favored weathervanes representing whales, ships, and mermaids. On churches the angel blowing a trumpet was very common. Our angel is a replica of a weathervane used in Massachusetts during the 1870's.

MATERIALS

1 Pine board ¾" x 10" x 20"
Dremel saw or hand coping saw
1 Pine base 4" x 4" x 6"
1 17" Straight lamp pipe, threaded both ends
1 Tube each of acrylic paints: cerulean blue,
black, white, and yellow ochre pale
1 V-shaped wood carving tool
Sand paper
1 Socket
1 Harp
1 1/8" Bushing inlet
1 8' parallel lamp cord
1 Felt pad
1 Doweling jig
1 Shade of your choice
1 Finial

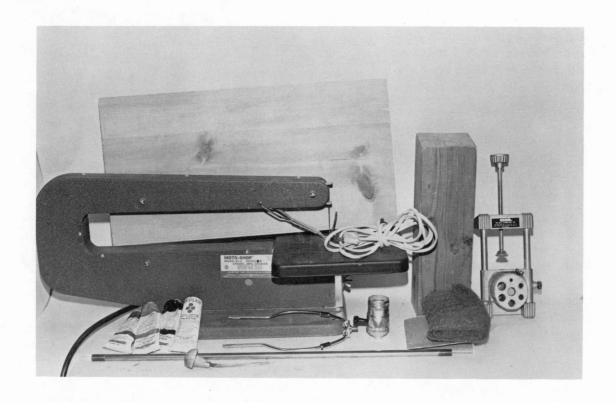

DIRECTIONS

STEP 1

STEP 1 -- Enlarge weathervane diagram and trace on a piece of ¾" clear pine. This can be easily and quickly cut with a Dremel Moto-shop saw or a coping saw. C-clamps will hold your saw securely to your work table.

STEP 2 -- Sand entire weathervane. Round off all edges. The outlines of the hair, hands, belt and shoes may be better defined by using a V-shaped wood cutting tool.

STEP 3 -- Paint entire weathervane with a coat of white acrylic. Let dry and paint the hair feet, horn, and belt black. The dress is painted cerulean blue. The face, hands, and feet are painted a pale yellow ochre.

STEP 4 -- When the paint dries, take a piece of fine steel wool and rub the entire weathervane until parts of the white undercoat and wood start to show through. This will give your weathervane an antique patina.

STEP 5 -- With a 3/8" drill bit, bore 2" hole into lamp base. Use doweling jig to assure a straight hole. Drill bushing inlet hole to meet center hole. Counterbore bottom to aid in wire insertion.

STEP 4

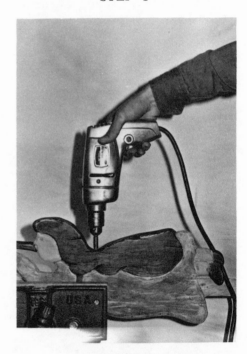

STEP 6

STEP 6 -- Drill hole with 3/8" bit through weathervane and insert lamp pipe. Contact cement will secure the weathervane to the pipe.

STEP 7 -- Insert lamp cord through bushing inlet and up through the center hole. Pass wire through lamp pipe and then screw threaded end of pipe into base. Base can be painted to match one of the colors of the angel.

STEP 8 -- Wire cord to socket.

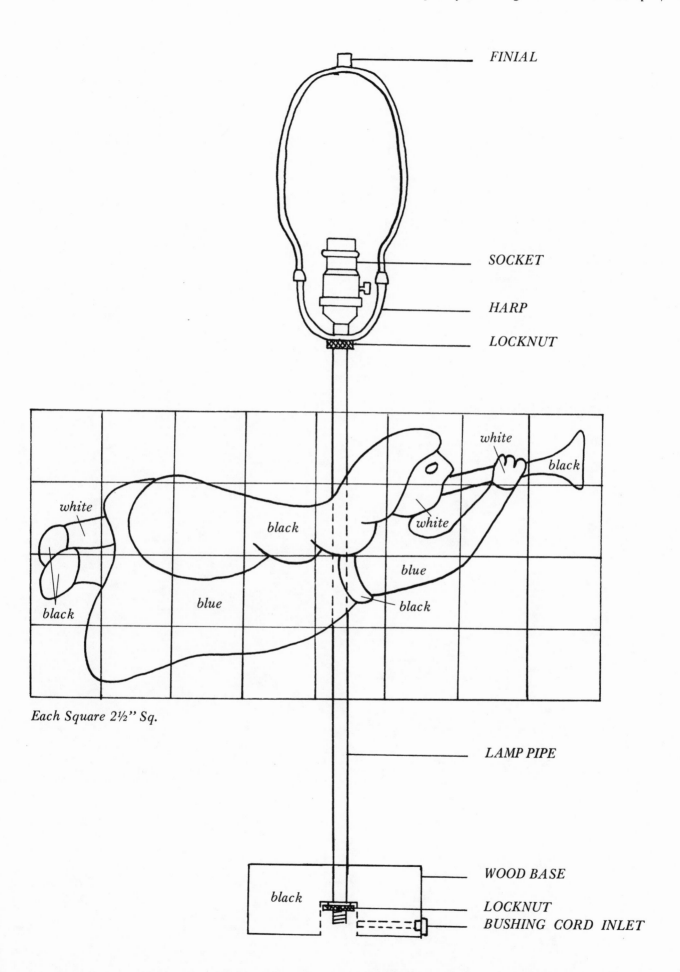

FINIAL

SOCKET

HARP

LOCKNUT

white

black

white

black

black

white

blue

blue

black

black

blue

Each Square 2½" Sq.

LAMP PIPE

WOOD BASE

black

LOCKNUT
BUSHING CORD INLET

ANTIQUE BOTTLE LAMP

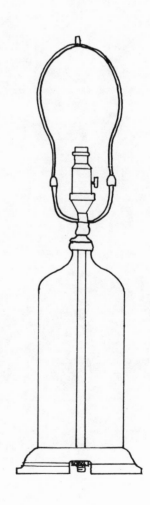

ANTIQUE BOTTLE LAMP

This project is an imaginative example of a
"found" item turned lamp. The bottle is rather
old and was actually found at the bottom of a
discarded box.

MATERIALS

1 Antique bottle or one of your choice
1 Straight lamp pipe to fit bottle, threaded both ends
1 Brass vase cap to fit bottle top
1 Neck beaded
1 Socket
1 Harp
1 Parallel lamp cord, 6'
1 Wooden round base
2 Locknuts
1 .3/8" glass drill bit
1 Felt pad
1 Shade of your choice
1 Finial

DIRECTIONS

STEP 1 -- Drill hole in the bottom center of bottle with the aid of a glass drill bit.

STEP 2 -- Drill hole in center of wooden base and counterbore underside to accommodate locknut. Drill horizontal hole for cord inlet.

STEP 3 -- Insert pipe through bottle and wood base. Secure with locknut. Place brass vase cap over bottle top and pipe. Secure to pipe with threaded neck.

STEP 4 -- Insert wire through base and pipe, and connect to socket.

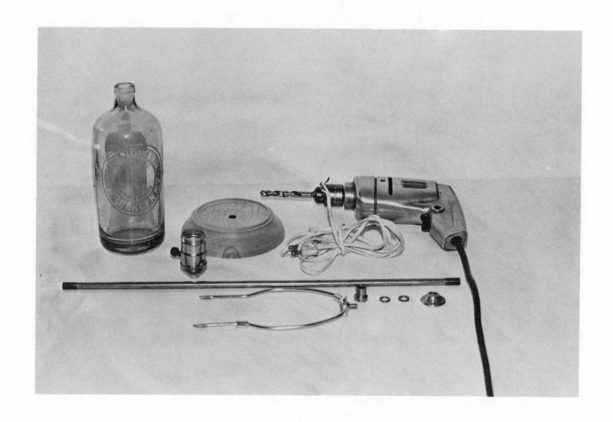

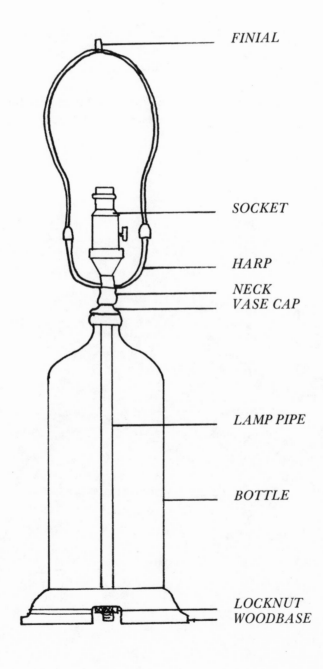

FINIAL

SOCKET

HARP

NECK
VASE CAP

LAMP PIPE

BOTTLE

LOCKNUT
WOODBASE

PERUVIAN GOURD LAMP

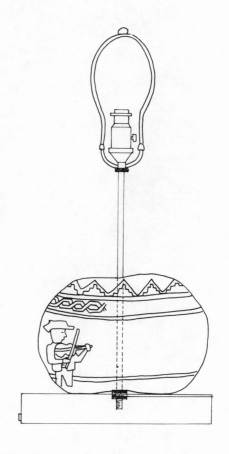

PERUVIAN GOURD LAMP

Peruvian craftsmen are well-known for their textiles, pottery and carvings. This carved gourd from Peru is another example of an unusual, but inexpensive object converted into a handsome lamp. Decorative gourds like this one are sold in stores that carry African or South American handicrafts.

MATERIALS

Carved gourd
" Spun brass base
Socket
Harp
Parallel lamp cord 8"
" Lamp pipe, threaded both ends
Locknuts
Finial

DIRECTIONS

STEP 1 -- Drill 3/8" hole in gourd top and bottom.

STEP 2 -- Screw first locknut onto threaded end of pipe base. Insert pipe into hole in base and secure with second locknut.

STEP 3 -- Place gourd onto lamp pipe.

STEP 4 -- Insert wire through pipe and connect to socket. Secure harp in place and select shade.

1. DRILLING HOLE IN GOURD

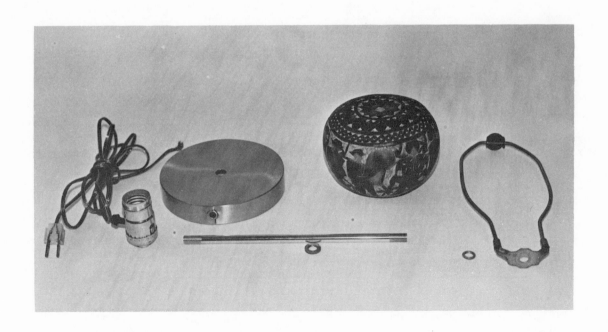

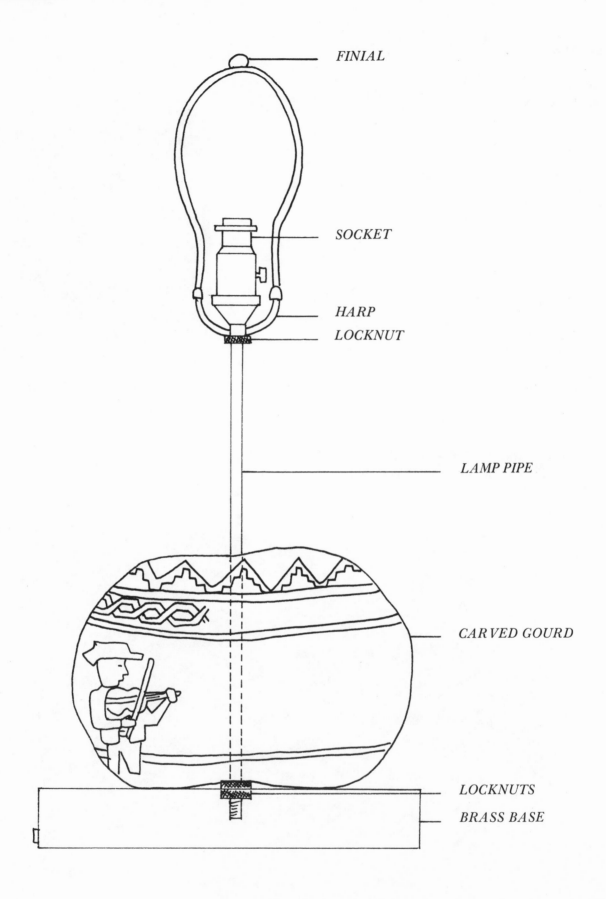

FINIAL

SOCKET

HARP

LOCKNUT

LAMP PIPE

CARVED GOURD

LOCKNUTS

BRASS BASE

COPPER TEAPOT LAMP

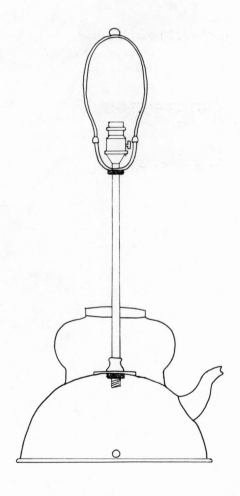

COPPER TEAPOT LAMP

A humble teapot makes a wonderful lamp.
This is an easy project that will complement any
decor.

DIRECTIONS

STEP 1 -- On some pots, the lid can be used instead of a brass vase cap. Unscrew the wooden top and enlarge screw opening if necessary. The pipe is connected to teapot lid or base cap with a threaded beaded neck and locknut.

STEP 2 -- Drill hole in back side of teapot for insertion of cord.

STEP 3 -- Insert wire through base and through lamp pipe.

STEP 4 -- Connect wire to socket.

STEP 5 -- Adhere brass cap or teapot lid to pot with contact cement.

NOTE: If you have a teapot with a rounded base, it will be necessary to secure pot to a wooden base with a screw.

MATERIALS

1 Copper teapot
1 Brass vase cap to fit over top opening of teapot
1 Straight lamp pipe, threaded both ends, 10"
1 Beaded neck
2 Locknuts
1 Socket
1 Harp
1 Parallel lamp cord 8'
Contact cement
1 Shade of your choice
1 Finial

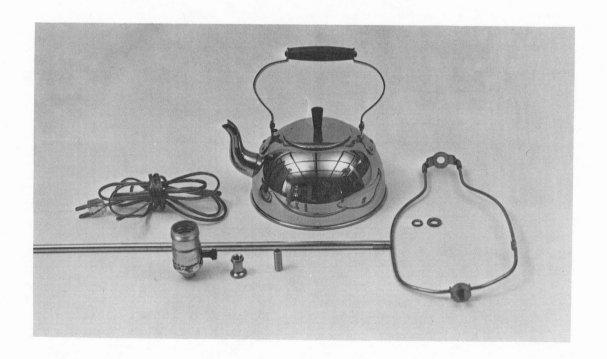

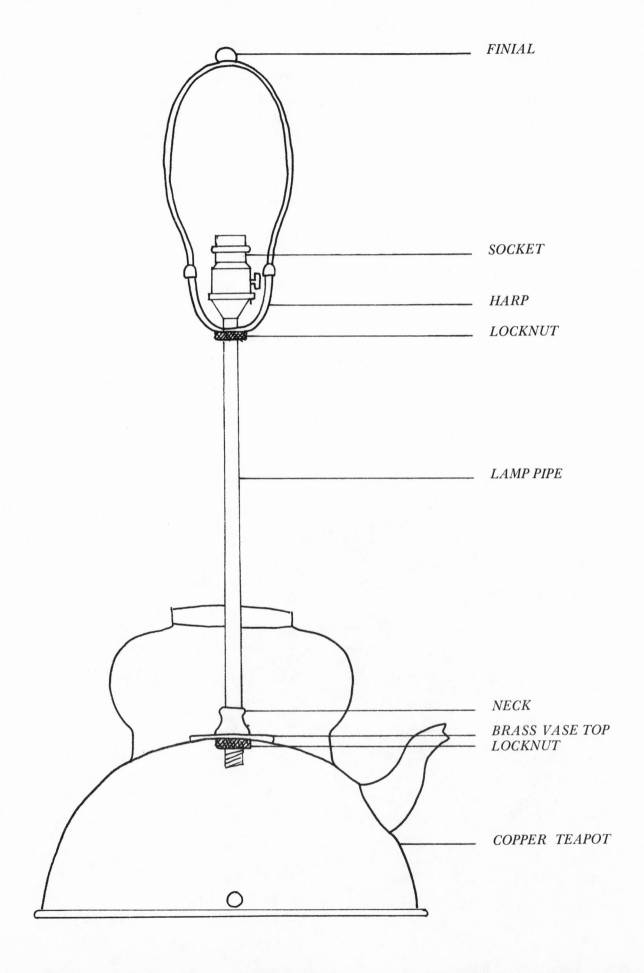

FINIAL

SOCKET

HARP

LOCKNUT

LAMP PIPE

NECK

BRASS VASE TOP
LOCKNUT

COPPER TEAPOT

ELECTRIC HURRICANE LAMP

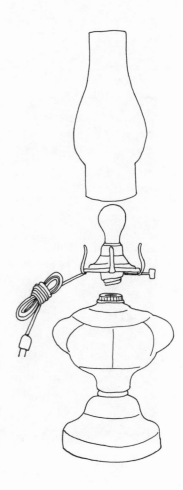

ELECTRIC HURRICANE LAMP

The beauty and simplicity of a hurricane
lamp can grace any room in the house. Just put
together a base and globe of your choice, even
using different glass colors and textures for each
part. The combination can make a terrific lamp!

MATERIALS

1 Glass Hurricane Lamp
1 Wired oil lamp converter

DIRECTIONS

STEP 1 -- Remove the wick part of the lamp
base, and replace it with wired oil lamp converter.

STEP 2 -- Replace chimney and plug into socket.

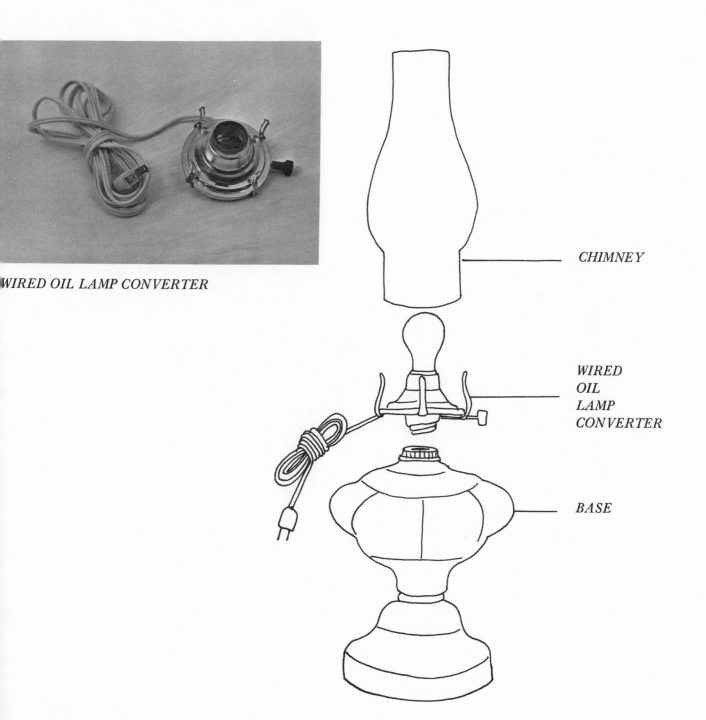

WIRED OIL LAMP CONVERTER

CHIMNEY

*WIRED
OIL
LAMP
CONVERTER*

BASE

ANTIQUE
COFFEE GRINDER LAMP

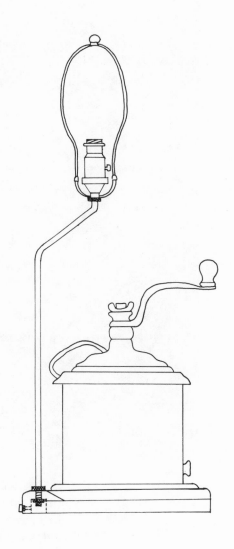

ANTIQUE COFFEE GRINDER LAMP

The selection and treatment of an item is very
important in lampmaking. This coffee grinder
gives a certain country flavor to any surrounding.
And, what a great gift for a coffee lover!

MATERIALS

1 Hand coffee grinder
1 Pine base ¾" x 8" x 8"
1 10" figurine bend lamp pipe
2 Locknuts
1 Socket
1 Harp
1 Parallel lamp cord 8'
1 Felt pad
½ pint of oil wood stain
1 Shade of your choice
1 Finial

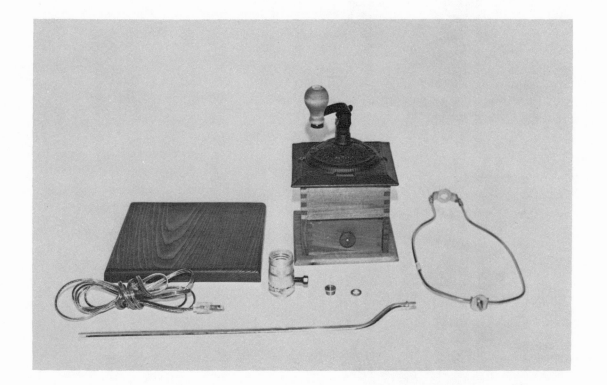

STEP 2

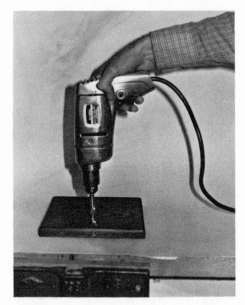

STEP 3

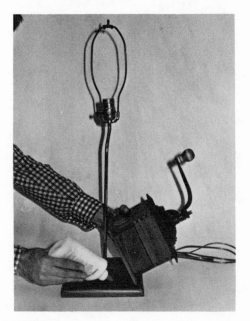

STEP 4

DIRECTIONS

STEP 1 -- Procure a hand coffee grinder.

STEP 2 -- Cut wood base for coffee grinder. Sand base, and stain.

STEP 3 -- Drill 3/8" hole in base back for bent arm pipe and cord inlet.

STEP 4 -- Affix coffee grinder to wood base with white wood glue.

STEP 5 -- Insert lamp pipe into base. Insert wire and connect to socket.

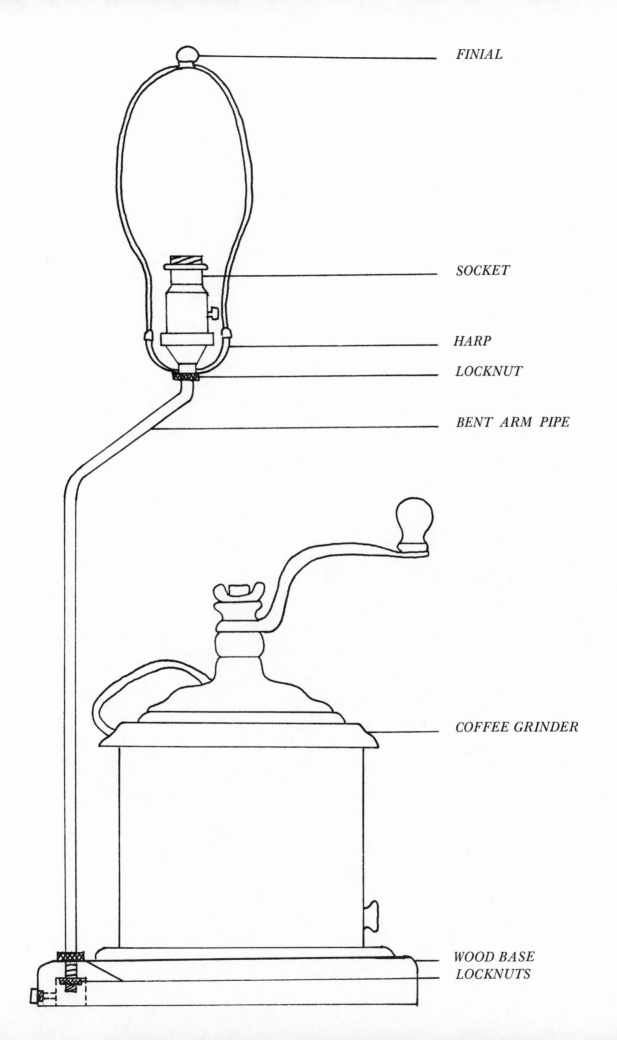

FINIAL

SOCKET

HARP

LOCKNUT

BENT ARM PIPE

COFFEE GRINDER

WOOD BASE
LOCKNUTS

CERAMIC   LAMP

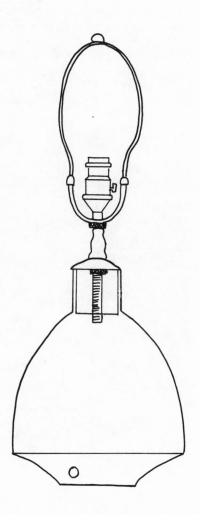

CERAMIC LAMP

Create a classic lamp from a simple clay pot.
This pot, part of a collection made by the authors,
was selected for its shapely design.

MATERIALS

1 Ceramic base
3/8" masonary drill bit
1 Brass vase cap
1 Sheet of cork
2 Locknuts
1 Socket
1 Harp
1 4" nipple
1 Parallel lamp cord 6'
1 Beaded neck
1 Felt pad
1 Shade of your choice
1 Finial

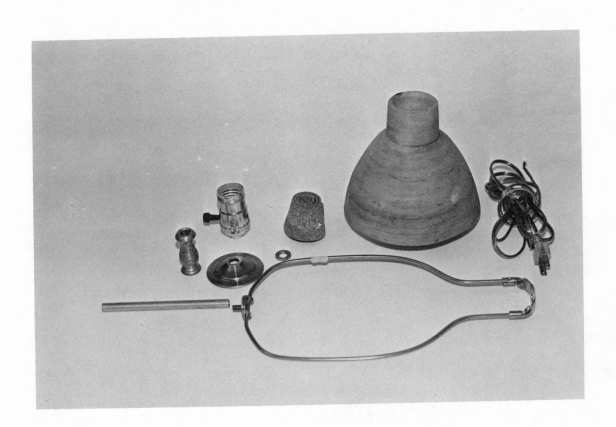

STEP 1

DIRECTIONS

STEP 1 -- With masonary drill bit, drill 3/8" hole in base for the insertion of the electrical cord.

STEP 2 -- Insert nipple through brass top, and connect with locknut on the underside of cap, and beaded neck on the top.

STEP 3 -- Insert lamp cord into the base and up through the nipple. Connect wire to socket.

STEP 4 -- Wrap enough cork around the nipple bottom to hold it in place when it is inserted into the top of vase.

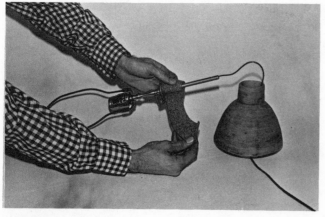

STEP 4

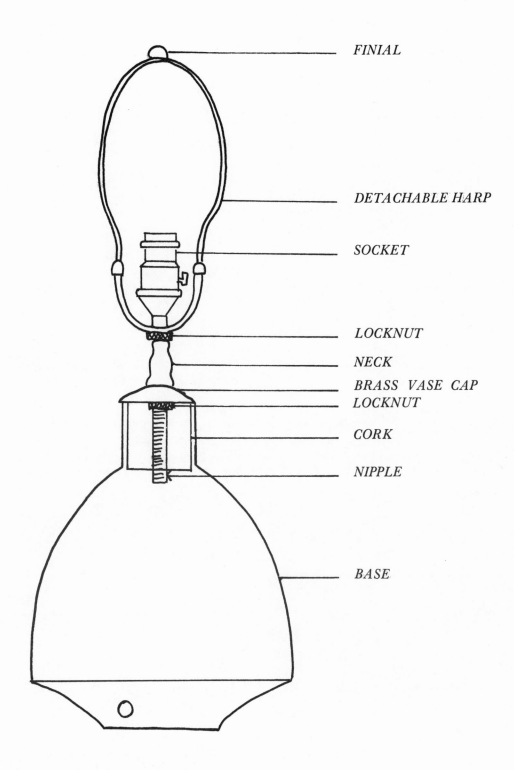

FINIAL

DETACHABLE HARP

SOCKET

LOCKNUT

NECK

BRASS VASE CAP

LOCKNUT

CORK

NIPPLE

BASE

EARLY AMERICAN
LANTERN LAMP

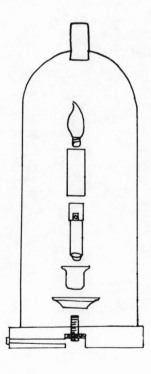

EARLY AMERICAN LANTERN LAMP

This project is a favorite of almost everyone
who sees it. A true example of a "new antique,"
this modernized lantern brings to mind the
simplicity and beauty of Early American design.

MATERIALS

Dremel saw, jig saw or coping saw
1 Pair small hinges
1 Door latch
4' of ½" pine
1 piece of sheet tin or aluminum, 5¾" x 9"
1 Nail punch and screwdriver
1 inch finishing nails
Upholsterer's tacks
1 Leather strip 1" x 14"
1 3½" Brass candle cup

1 Candle sleeve brass
1 Electric candle socket
1 Plastic candle sleeve
1 2" nipple
1 6' parallel lamp cord
1 Locknut
1 1/8" bushing inlet
1 Felt pad
½ pint of oil wood stain

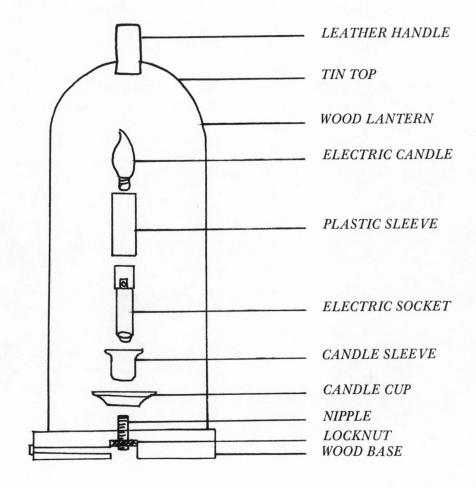

LEATHER HANDLE

TIN TOP

WOOD LANTERN

ELECTRIC CANDLE

PLASTIC SLEEVE

ELECTRIC SOCKET

CANDLE SLEEVE

CANDLE CUP

NIPPLE
LOCKNUT
WOOD BASE

DIRECTIONS

STEP 1

STEP 1 -- Cut wood, according to diagram, for lantern. Nail together with finishing nails and white glue.

STEP 2 -- Drill 3/8" hole in base for nipple and horizontal hole for wire inlet.

STEP 3

STEP 3 -- Measure and cut 5 ¾" x 9" piece of sheet tin. With nail punch and hammer, make holes in the tin. Place tin on a piece of soft pine lumber when hammering holes.

STEP 4

STEP 4 -- Affix tin top to the wooden lantern with upholsterer's tacks.

STEP 5 -- Insert nipple into base. Place candle cup and sleeve onto nipple. Then screw electric candle onto nipple. Insert wire through base and nipple, and wire to candle.

STEP 6

STEP 6 -- Stain lantern with oil wood stain.

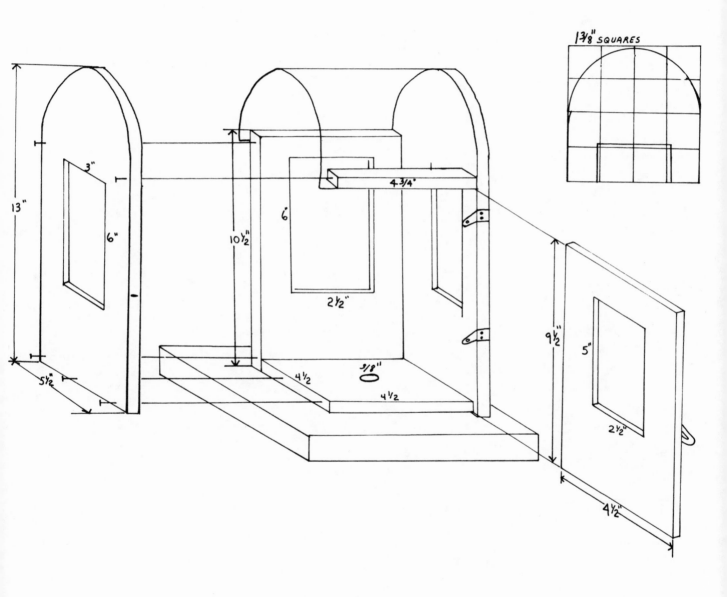

EARLY AMERICAN
CORNER LAMP

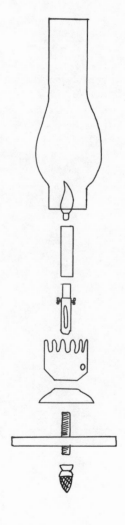

EARLY AMERICAN CORNER LAMP

Corner shelves are a decorative addition to
any interior, especially when they hold lamps.
An uncomplicated project to lighten up even the
darkest corner.

MATERIALS

2 ½' of ½" pine lumber
1 10" smoked glass chimney
1 3 ½" brass vase cap
1 2" nipple
1 Brass finial
1 Electric candle socket
1 Plastic candle sleeve
1 Parallel lamp cord 6'
1 ON - OFF Cord Switch
Sandpaper
Dremel saw or coping saw
½ Pint oil wood stain

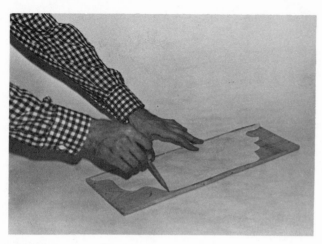

STEP 1

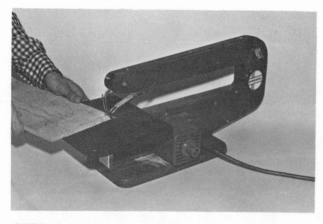

STEP 2

DIRECTIONS

STEP 1 -- Enlarge patterns and trace onto wood. With dremel saw cut out designs.

STEP 2 -- Sand wood.

STEP 3 Stain with oil wood stain. Let dry.

STEP 4 -- Put lamp holder together with wood glue and small nails.

STEP 5 -- Drill 3/8" hole for insertion of nipple. Drill hole in the back corner for the cord inlet.

STEP 6 -- Insert nipple and assemble chimney hardware onto nipple.

STEP 7 -- Screw candle socket onto nipple. Insert wire through cord inlet and through hole in brass chimney holder, and connect wire to socket.

STEP 8 -- Connect ON - OFF switch to lamp cord following manufacturer's instructions.

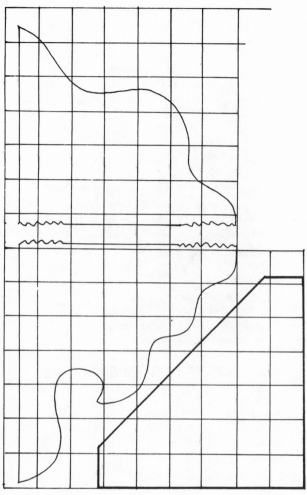

Each Square 1" Sq.

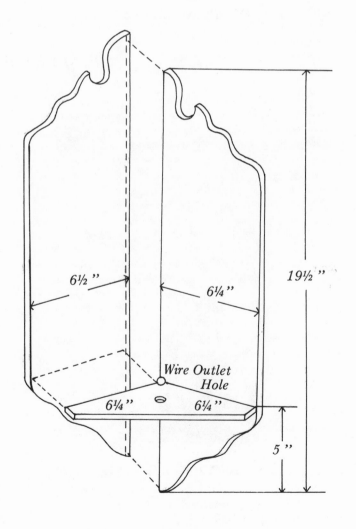

6½"

6¼"

19½"

*Wire Outlet
Hole*

6¼"

6¼"

5"

1. INSERTING NIPPLE

2. CHIMNEY AND BRASS CAP

CHIMNEY HARDWARE ASSEMBLY

3. ELECTRIC SOCKET

4. CHIMNEY

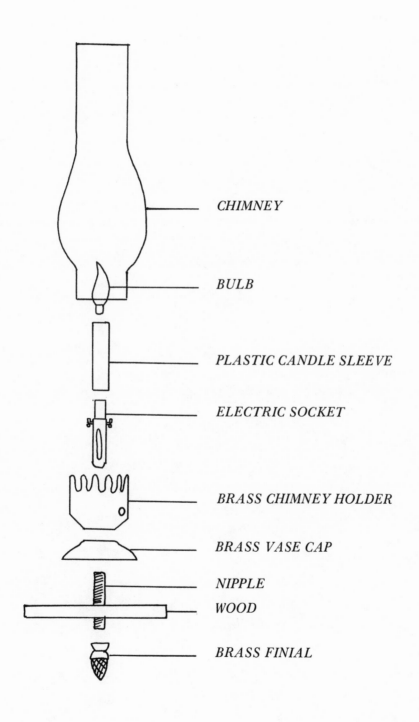

CHIMNEY

BULB

PLASTIC CANDLE SLEEVE

ELECTRIC SOCKET

BRASS CHIMNEY HOLDER

BRASS VASE CAP

NIPPLE

WOOD

BRASS FINIAL

GOLD LEAF STENCILED LAMP

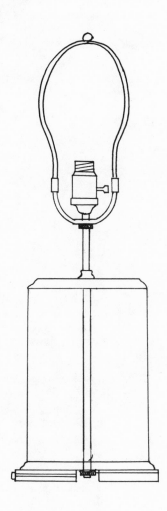

GOLD LEAF STENCILED LAMP

Stenciling is a fascinating art -- Early
Americans also used it on walls, mantlepieces and
furniture. Here's a quick, mistake-proof way to
stencil a lamp using goldleaf on black paint.

MATERIALS

½ " Plywood: 2 pieces 7" x 9" (A)
           2 pieces 2" x 9" (B)
           1 piece 9" x 3" (C)
           5' of ½ " Cove molding (D)
           1 piece 8 ½ " x 4 ½ " (E)
½ pt. Flat black paint and ½ " paint brush
½ pt. Varnish and ½ " varnish brush
Stencil paper
Bronze powder -- 1 Tube
1 Socket

1 Parallel lamp cord
1 Harp
13" Straight brass lamp pipe -- threaded both ends
Locknuts
Neck
1/8 " Bushing inlet
Miter box
1" Finishing nails
1 Finial

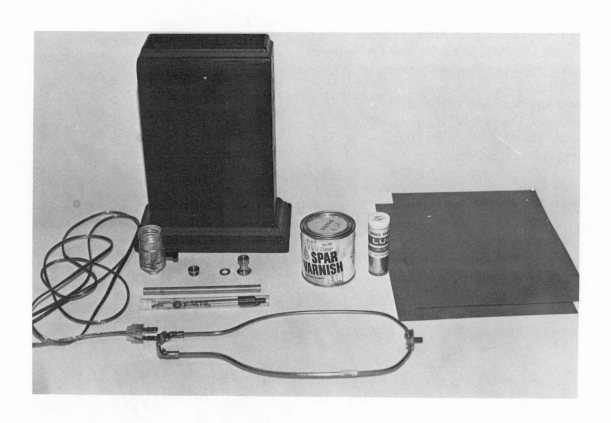

DIRECTIONS

STEP 1 -- Follow pattern for making lamp base. Base is made of ½" pine or plywood. Half-inch cove molding is cut and mitered to fit around the top and bottom of the lamp base.

STEP 2 -- Nail base together, set and fill all nail holes. Then sand base smooth.

STEP 3 -- Give base two coats of flat black paint and allow to dry thoroughly.

STEP 4 -- The stencils are given full size. Trace these onto a piece of vellum paper. Place design on top of stencil paper and trace over design. Its imprint will be left on the stencil paper. Using an Exacto knife or razor blade, cut out each piece of the stencil. The secret of a fine cut stencil, is to have clean-cut edges. Stencil paper can be bought at most art supply stores.

STEP 5 -- Give the entire lamp base a thin even coat of varnish. Let varnish dry until it is slightly sticky when touched with a finger. Drying time will vary according to the weather.

STEP 6 -- Place small amount of bronze powder onto a piece of velvet. A second small piece of velvet will be used to apply the bronze powder.

STEP 4

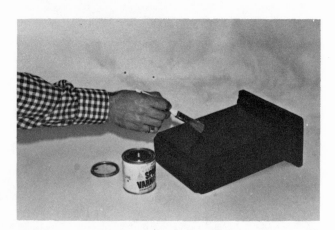

STEP 5

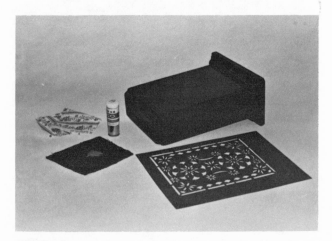

STEP 6

STEP 7 -- Place lamp base in a horizontal position. Lay your stencil down on the front of the base, and press down lightly until it adheres to the varnish. (See Photo)

STEP 7

STEP 8 -- Put velvet over index finger and dip into bronze powder. (Lightly tap finger to remove any excess powder). Apply only a small amount of powder to stencil at a time. With a circular motion build up the desired brightness. Stenciled parts should have a uniform appearance. Remove any excess powder on stencil before lifting it off.

STEP 9 -- Clean stencil off with turpentine and repeat Step 8 for the back. The sides are done exactly the same as the front. Any mistakes can be fixed by painting over the bronze powder with the flat black paint used for background.

STEP 8

STEP 10 -- Allow base to dry for at least 48 hours, or until the powder is dry. Remove any excess powder with a piece of damp cloth. Then paint entire base with a coat of varnish. Let this dry, and apply a second coat of varnish. Let dry.

STEP 11 -- Drill 3/8" hole in top of base and through the bottom. Counterbore the bottom to put locknut on. Drill horizontal cord inlet hole.

STEP 12 -- Insert lamp pipe and secure with locknut and neck. Insert wire and connect to socket.

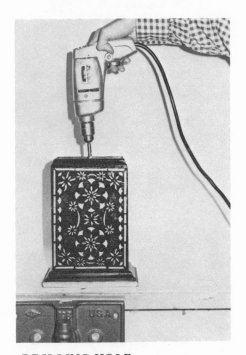

DRILLING HOLE

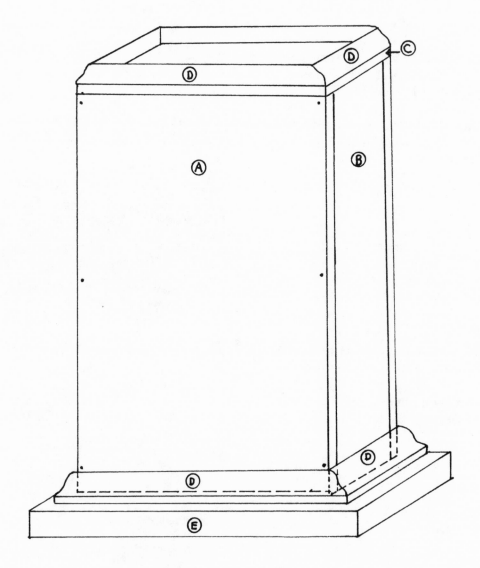

STENCIL GIVEN ACTUAL SIZE FRONT STENCIL

FULL SIZE STENCIL SIDE

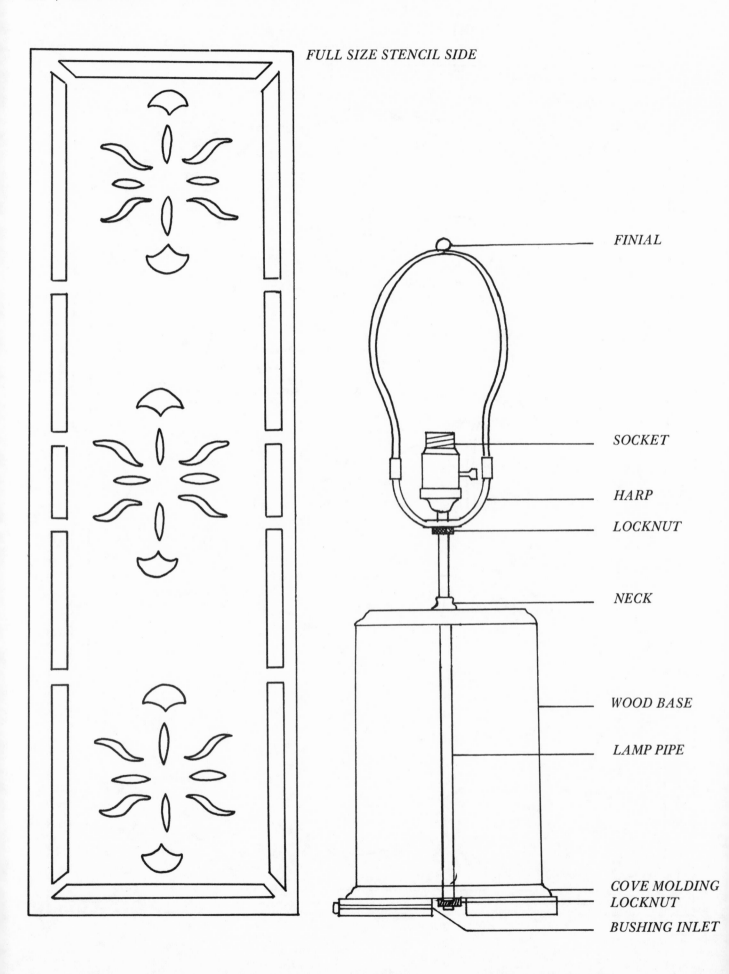

FINIAL

SOCKET

HARP

LOCKNUT

NECK

WOOD BASE

LAMP PIPE

COVE MOLDING
LOCKNUT

BUSHING INLET

SEA FAN AND SHELLS LAMP

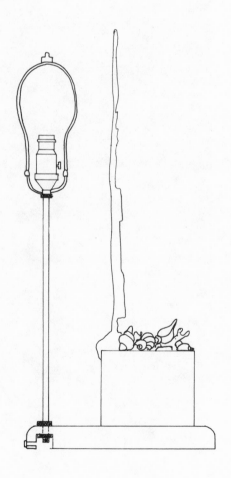

SEA FAN AND SHELLS LAMP

Did you collect shells at the beach last summer? Put them to good use, by making a one-of-a-kind lamp that will be a guaranteed conversation piece. For the beach house, for a gift or for yourself. (Clay pot courtesy of Michael Plant.)

MATERIALS

¾ " x 8" x 8" wooden base pine
1 Lamp pipe threaded ends only 8"
1 4" x 4" x 6" base for shells pine
Sea fan and shells
1 Socket, harp, and cord
1 Felt base pad
1 Bushing, cord outlet 1/8"
1 Shade of your choice
½ pt. Oil wood stain
1 Finial

DIRECTIONS

STEP 1 -- Cut wooden base, sand and stain a color of your choice. Cut piece of wood for shell base.

STEP 2 -- Drill hole for pipe and cord inlet. Insert pipe and secure with locknuts.

STEP 3 -- Glue sea fan to shell base and glue shells over the rest of the base.

STEP 4 -- Glue shell base to lamp base.

STEP 5 -- Insert wire through lamp pipe and connect to socket.

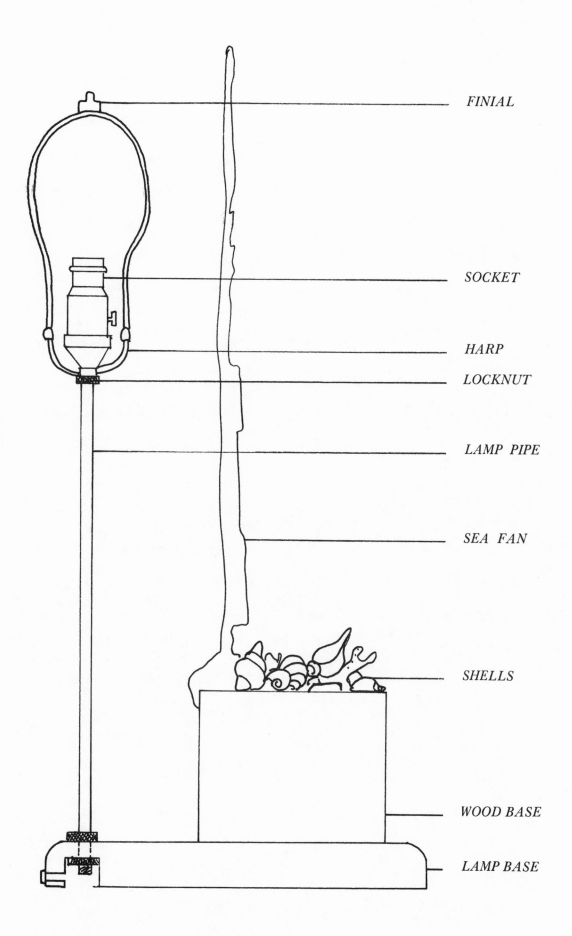

FINIAL

SOCKET

HARP

LOCKNUT

LAMP PIPE

SEA FAN

SHELLS

WOOD BASE

LAMP BASE

ORIENTAL BASKET LAMP

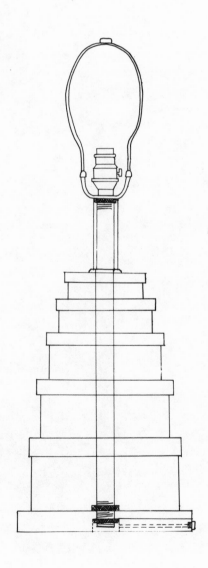

ORIENTAL BASKET LAMP

Graduated sizes of inexpensive baskets are piled on top of one another to make an oriental-looking lamp. Very simple, very inexpensive and very easy to make.

MATERIALS

1 8" diameter wooden base
5 Graduated baskets
1 18" Straight brass lamp pipe threaded both ends
3 Locknuts
1 2½ " Brass vase cap
1 1/8" Bushing inlet
1 8' Parallel lamp cord
1 Socket
1 Harp
1 5" Brass neck pipe spacer
1 Felt base pad
1 Shade of your choice
1 Finial

DIRECTIONS

STEP 1 -- Cut a small hole, large enough for the running thread pipe to pass through, into the top and bottom center of each basket.

STEP 2 -- A round wooden base was cut to form the base. Drill hole into center to provide for the wire and pipe. Counterbore the bottoms and drill horizontal wire holes.

STEP 3 -- Next install the electrical parts, hardware and a felt base.

STEP 4 -- Select an appropriate shade.

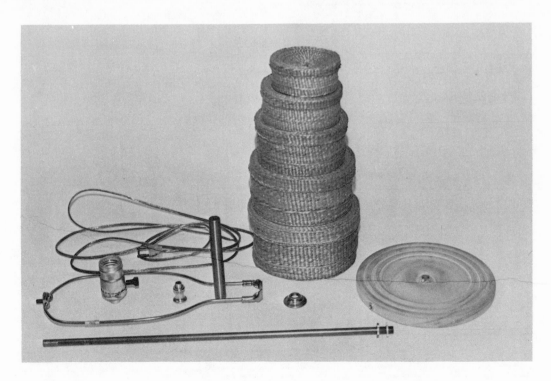

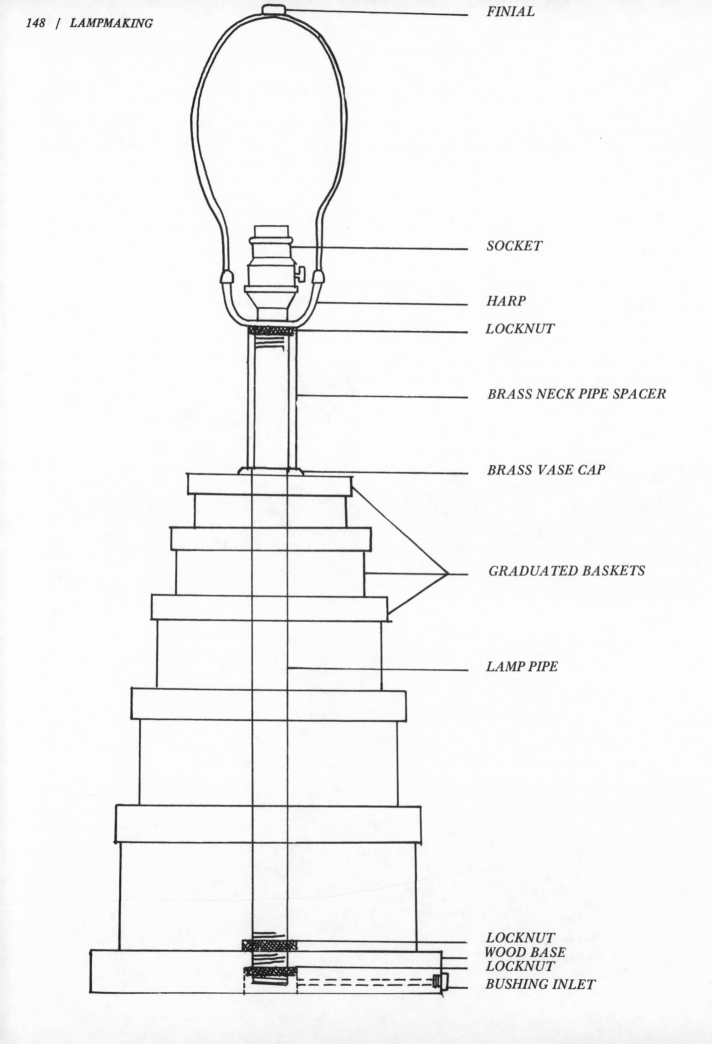

FINIAL

SOCKET

HARP

LOCKNUT

BRASS NECK PIPE SPACER

BRASS VASE CAP

GRADUATED BASKETS

LAMP PIPE

LOCKNUT
WOOD BASE
LOCKNUT
BUSHING INLET

RATTAN COVERED LAMP

RATTAN COVERED LAMP

A simple cardboard mailing tube, an
inexpensive rattan place mat and a few lamp
parts is all you need for a real eye-catcher of a
lamp. It can be put together in just a few hours.

MATERIALS

1 4½" diameter heavy duty mailing tube 12"long
1 4½" brass vase top
1 Rattan place mat
1 14" Straight brass lamp pipe threaded both ends
1 6" Spun brass base
1 Harp
1 Socket
1 8' parallel lamp cord
1 Shade of your choice

DIRECTIONS

STEP 1 -- A heavy duty mailing tube makes up this base. Around this is glued a rattan place mat. Use super strength glue. Rubberbands will hold the mat in place while it dries.

STEP 2 -- A spun brass vase top and plain brass base make up the top and bottom of the lamp.

STEP 3 -- Install all hardware and electrical parts as shown in the drawings.

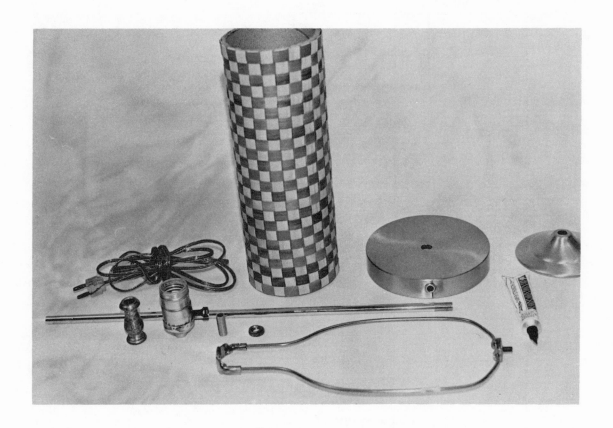

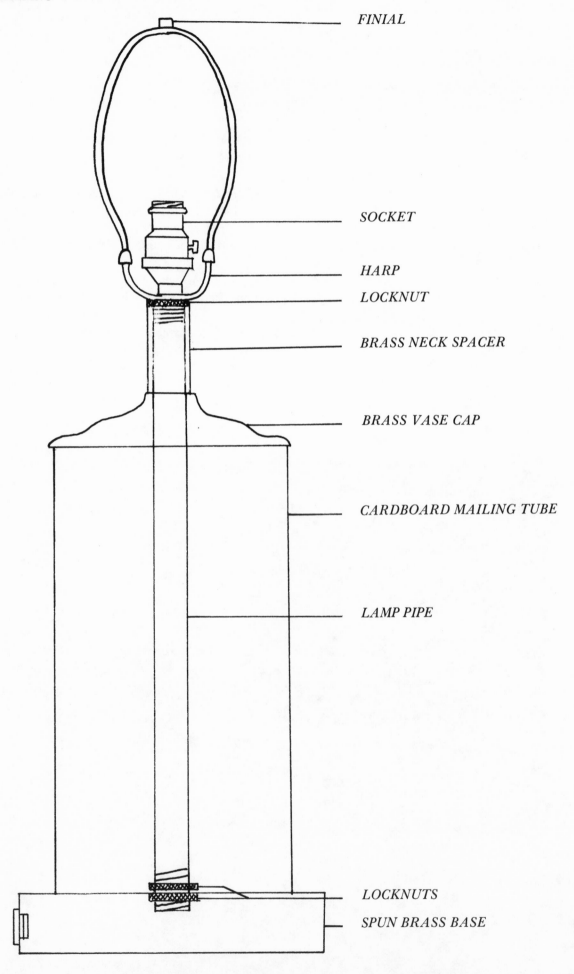

FINIAL

SOCKET

HARP

LOCKNUT

BRASS NECK SPACER

BRASS VASE CAP

CARDBOARD MAILING TUBE

LAMP PIPE

LOCKNUTS

SPUN BRASS BASE

WOOD AND BRASS
HANGING REFLECTOR CHANDELIER

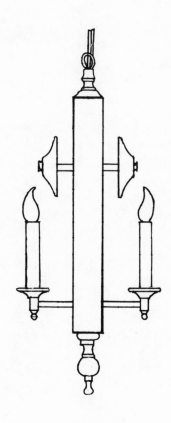

WOOD AND BRASS HANGING REFLECTOR
CHANDELIER

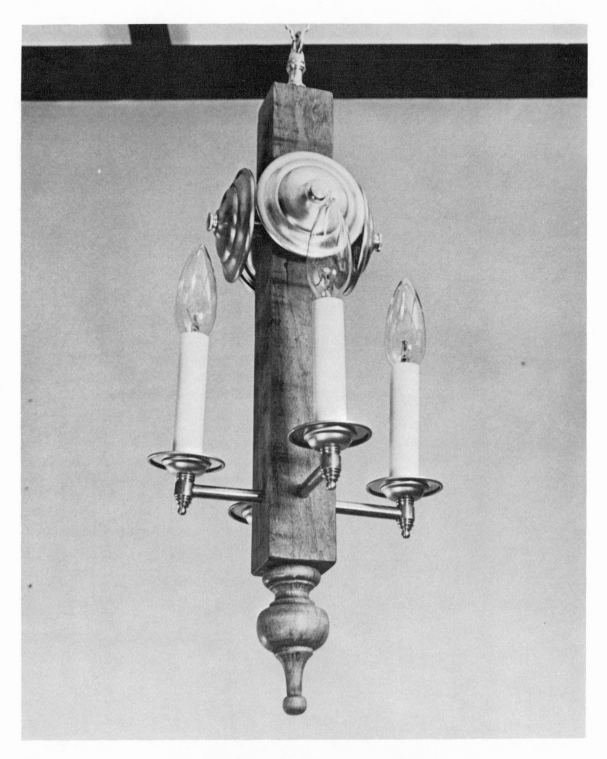

Reflector lamps were used in colonial times
when more light was desired. This wood and
brass reflector chandelier combines the qualities
of reflectors and chandeliers, for a truly decorative
lamp.

MATERIALS

1 2 ” x 2 ” x 15 ” cherry wood center pole
4 3½ ” pieces of plain soft brass pipe 1/8 ” ip
4 2½ ” pieces of plain soft brass pipe 1/8 ” ip
4 2¼ ” brass candle cups
4 3½ ” brass reflectors (brass vase caps)
4 Knurled brass caps Tapped 1/8 ”
4 Brass 90° angle nozzles
4 Electric candle sockets
4 Plastic candle covers
4 ½ ” nipples

1 6 ’ parallel lamp cord
1 Turned wood finial
1 Lamp chain
Tap and die wrench 1/8 ” ip die
Doweling jig
Solderless connectors
½ Pint oil wood stain
1 Brass loop
1 2 ” Nipple

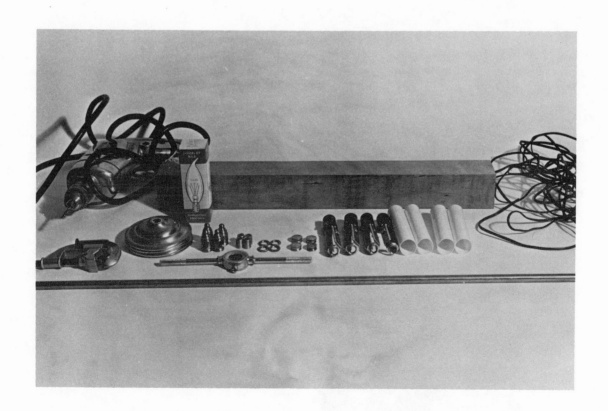

DIRECTIONS

STEP 2

STEP 1 -- Sand cherry wood center smooth and stain.

STEP 2 -- With the aid of a doweling jig, measure and drill holes for the candle arms, reflectors, and center hole. Counterbore bottom to allow for connection of wires.

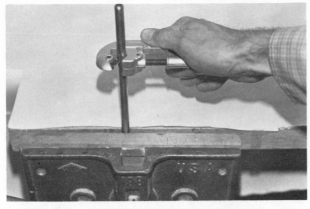

STEP 3

STEP 3 -- Cut four pieces of pipe 3½ ", and four pieces 2½ " long. With the aid of the tap and die wrench thread one end of each piece of pipe.

STEP 3

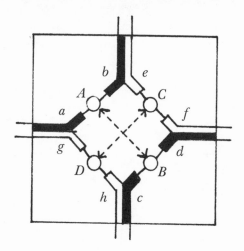

WIRING DIAGRAM

STEP 4 -- Following the diagram, assemble and wire the four candle arms.

STEP 5 -- Insert wires into center pole, and connect wires following diagram.

Connect a to b at A

Connect c to d at B

Connect e to f at C

Connect g to h at D

Connect A to B and C to D

Now, instead of eight separate wires, you will have only two wires. These two wires are then connected to the wire that runs from the ceiling outlet, down through the center of chandelier, to connect with the other two wires. Connect wires with solderless connectors, soldering iron, or electrical tape.

STEP 6 -- Insert candle arms into wood center pole, and secure with a small amount of contact cement.

STEP 7 -- Secure wooden finial to the bottom of wooden center pole with wood glue.

STEP 8 -- Assemble reflector cups and insert into center pole. Secure to pole with contact cement.

STEP 9 -- Connect brass loop onto top of pole with a threaded 2 " nipple. Connect lamp chain to loop and run wire through chain.

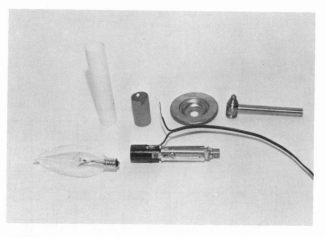

STEP 4

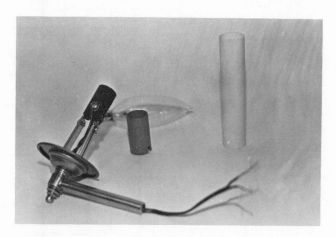

STEP 4

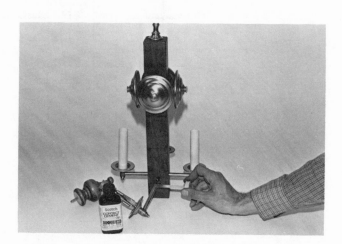

STEP 6

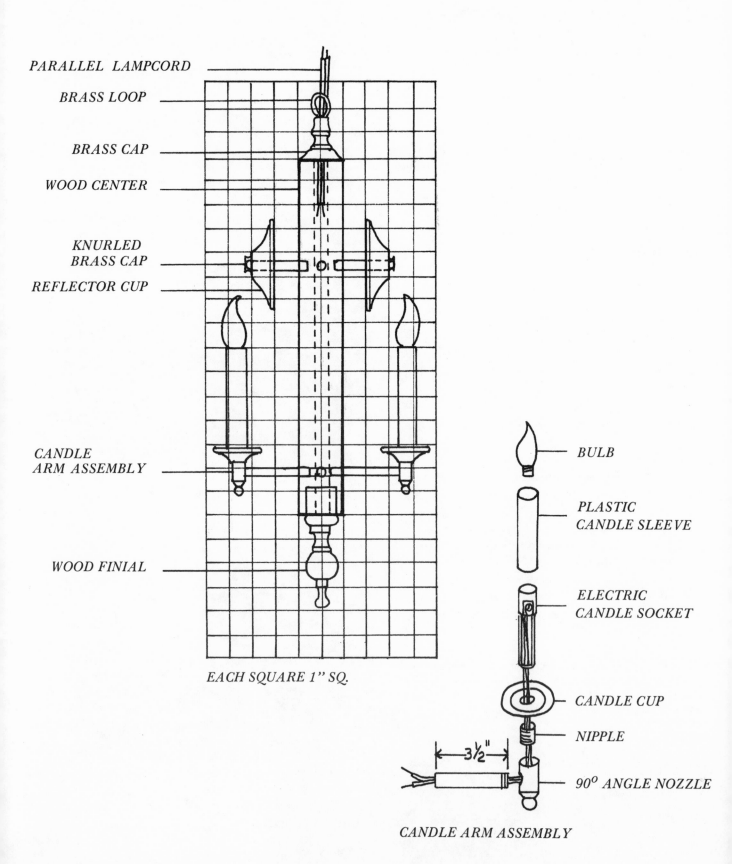

PARALLEL LAMPCORD

BRASS LOOP

BRASS CAP

WOOD CENTER

KNURLED
BRASS CAP

REFLECTOR CUP

CANDLE
ARM ASSEMBLY

WOOD FINIAL

EACH SQUARE 1" SQ.

BULB

PLASTIC
CANDLE SLEEVE

ELECTRIC
CANDLE SOCKET

CANDLE CUP

NIPPLE

3½"

90° ANGLE NOZZLE

CANDLE ARM ASSEMBLY

EARLY AMERICAN
TIN CHANDELIER

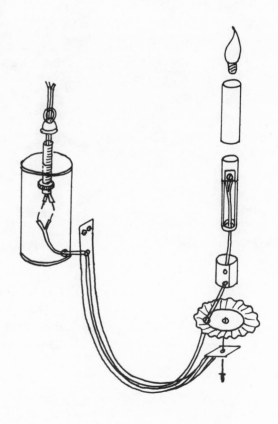

EARLY AMERICAN TIN CHANDELIER
(ELECTRIC)

You can add that missing touch of Americana to your home with this tin chandelier. Its flowing arms and flat black finish will make this lamp a real collector's piece.

MATERIALS

Tin can 5½" high 2½" diameter
4 Aluminum candle cups
No. 18 Guage sheet aluminum
Rubber hammer
Scissors or Tin Snips
Rivet gun
Liquid solder
Wire and electric candles
Pan 7" diameter
Scotch Super Strength Glue
Flat black spray paint -- 1 can
Loop 1", Nipple and 1 lock washer
Chain
Wire connectors

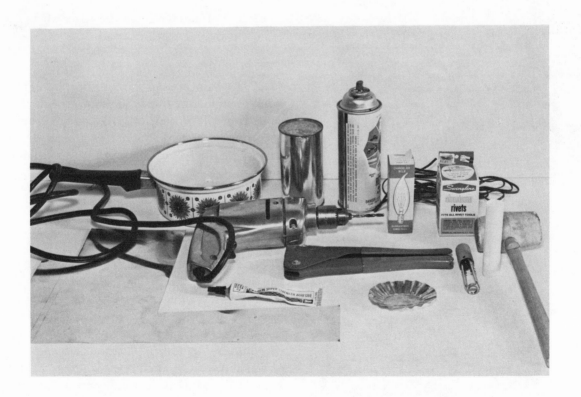

DIRECTIONS

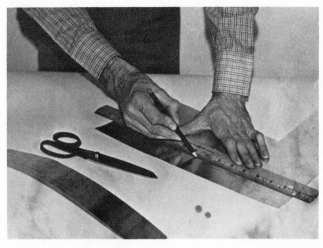

STEP 1

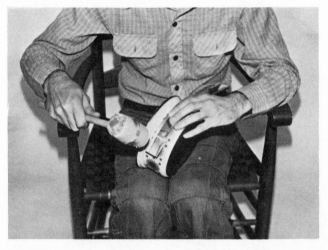

STEP 3

STEP 4

STEP 1 -- Measure and cut tin for the four arms.

STEP 2 – Hammer down the edges of the arm as in photo for 16 arm chandelier.

STEP 3 -- Form arms around the pan. With the rubber hammer beat arm to shape around the pan. This will prevent any sharp bends from occurring in the tin. Practice on a piece of tin first to get the feel of forming the arm around the pan.

STEP 4 -- Drill hole into center of each candle cup, and along the edge for the wire. Drill hole in lamp arm for the candle cup. Then rivet cup to end of the arm. Drill two holes in the other end of arms to rivet to can, plus one to insert wire into inside of can. Position arm onto side of can and with a pencil mark where to drill holes into can. Drill first hole and rivet arm to can. Now make sure arm is in the right position and drill second hole into can and rivet. Next, drill hole into can for the wire.

STEP 4

STEP 5 -- Cut four pieces of tin for the candle sleeves. The edges needn't be bent down for the sleeves. Form the sleeve around a ¾ " dowel stick or a broom handle. Overlap the edges of the sleeve ¼ " and drill a hole into both edges of the sleeve. Leave sleeve on the dowel. When drilling the hole rivet sleeve together and drill a second hole for the wire at the bottom of the sleeve.

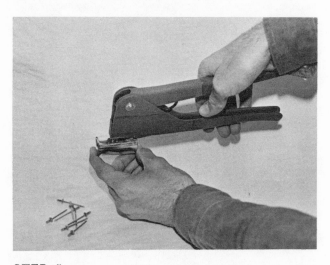

STEP 5

STEP 6 -- Wire the electric candles and run wire through the hole in the sleeve and then through the hole in the candle cup.

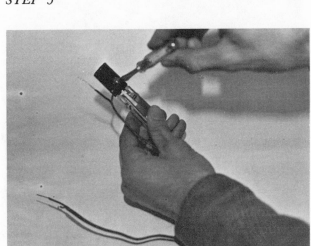

STEP 6

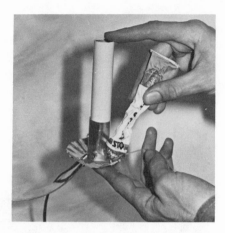

STEP 7

STEP 7 -- Solder sleeve to the cup with liquid solder. The candle sleeves can be held in place while drying with a piece of scotch tape.

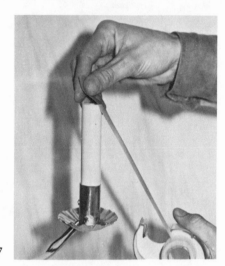

STEP 7

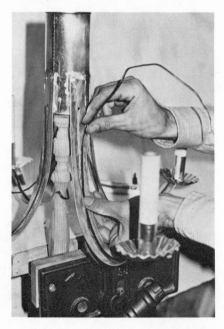

STEP 8

STEP 8 -- Glue wire down along the top of each arm.

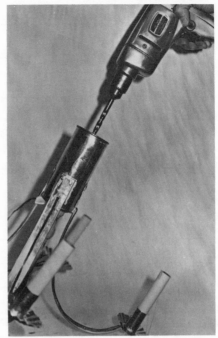

STEP 9 -- Drill 3/8 " hole in top of can. Bottom of can is cut out. Insert ½ " long nipple through hole. Screw loop onto nipple top and lock washer onto the underside of can. Connect wires together and run through nipple.

STEP 9

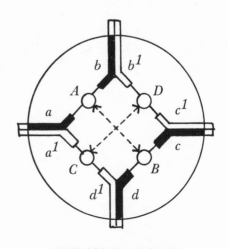

STEP 10 -- Paint entire lamp with flat black spray paint. Let dry and insert plastic candle sleeves and bulbs.

STEP 10

STEP 11 -- WIRING INSTRUCTIONS:

    Connect a to b at A

    Connect b^1 to c^1 at D

    Connect c to d at B

    Connect a^1 to d^1 at C

    Connect A to B and C to D

You will now have two wires when these wires are connected together. These two wires are then connected to the wire that runs from the ceiling outlet. Solder or use solderless connectors to secure wires together.

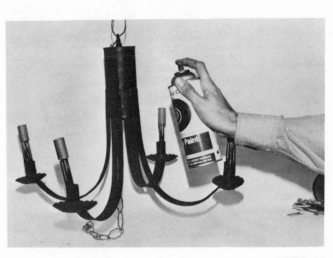

WIRING DIAGRAM

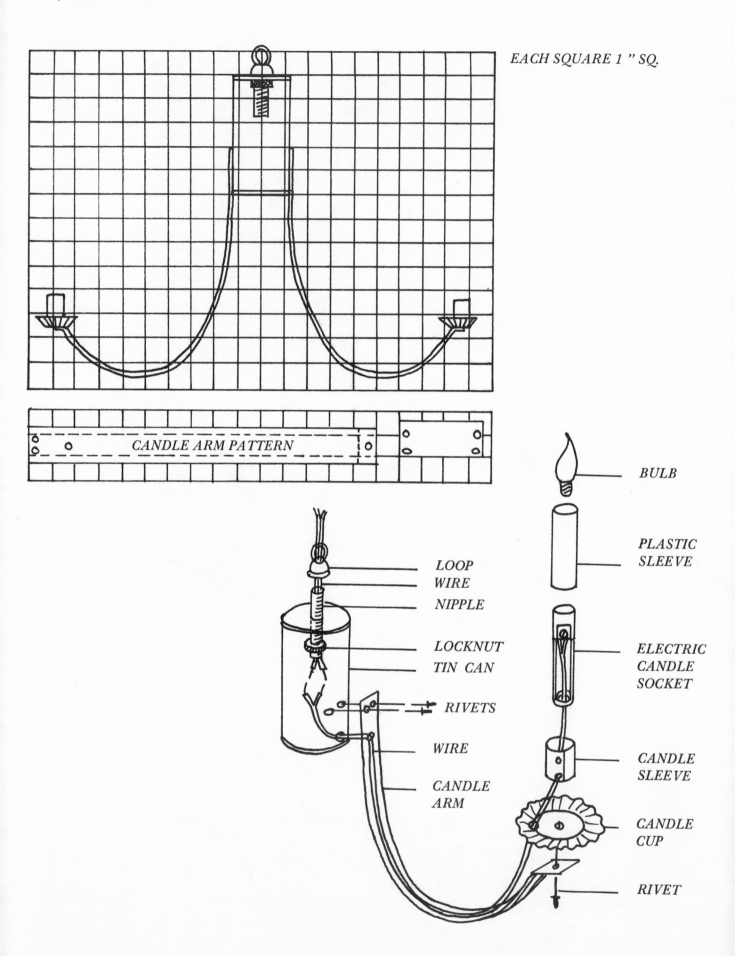

EACH SQUARE 1 " SQ.

CANDLE ARM PATTERN

BULB

PLASTIC
SLEEVE

LOOP
WIRE
NIPPLE

ELECTRIC
CANDLE
SOCKET

LOCKNUT
TIN CAN

RIVETS

CANDLE
SLEEVE

WIRE

CANDLE
ARM

CANDLE
CUP

RIVET

WOOD AND BRASS CHANDELIER

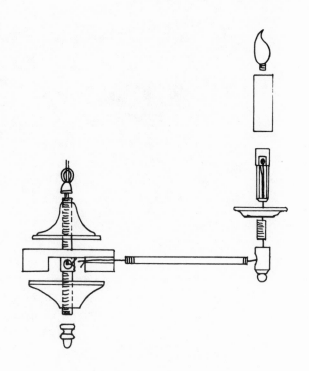

WOOD AND BRASS CHANDELIER

You will re-create the mood of candlelight with this chandelier. You would expect to pay up to a hundred dollars or more for this type of lamp in a store, but you will be able to make it for only a fraction of its true cost.

MATERIALS

1 5" Diameter wooden center
6 8" Straight brass pipe threaded both ends
6 90° Angle nozzles
6 3½" Brass candle cups
6 Electric candles and sleeves
6 ½" Nipples
2 Brass vase tops -- 4½" diameter

2 2" Nipples
1 Arm end nozzle
1 Finial
1 Brass loop
10 Feet of parallel lamp cord
Plastic solderless connectors
Doweling jig
Fixture chain

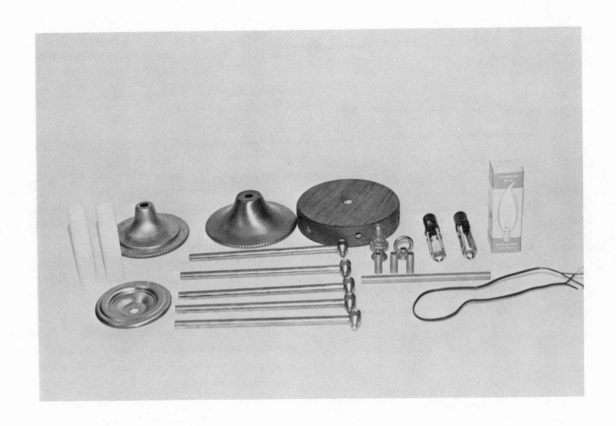

DIRECTIONS

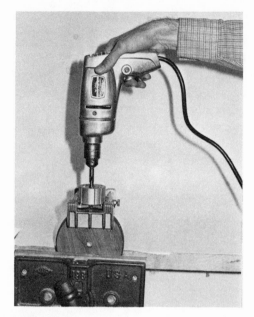

STEP 1

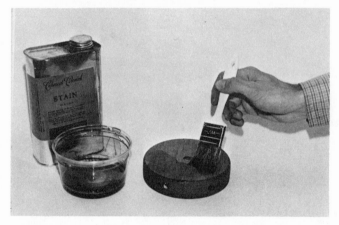

STEP 2

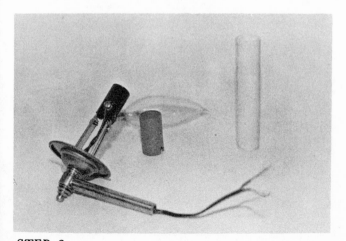

STEP 3

STEP 1 -- Drill 3/8" hole through wooden center. Next measure and drill six holes along the outer edge of center. Each hole should connect at center hole. A doweling jig will assure you of a straight hole in drilling. The underside of center can be routed out to make more room for connecting of wires.

STEP 2 -- Sand and stain center.

STEP 3 -- Wire electric candles and assemble the six arms as shown in diagram.

STEP 4 -- Assemble nipples through center and connect with arm end connector. Center wire is then inserted through nipple and out the side hole of the arm and connector. Connect center wire with electric candle wires with solderless connectors.

STEP 5 -- WIRING INSTRUCTIONS: Follow diagram and connect the six black wires together and the six white ones. You will now have two wires which are then connected to the wire that runs from the ceiling outlet.

STEP 6 -- Assemble brass tops over nipples and connect with finials on bottom and brass loop on top. Connect chain to loop and thread wire through chain.

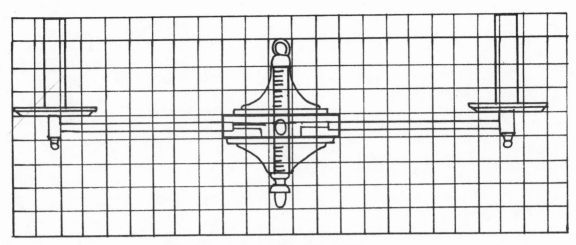

EACH SQUARE 1" SQ.

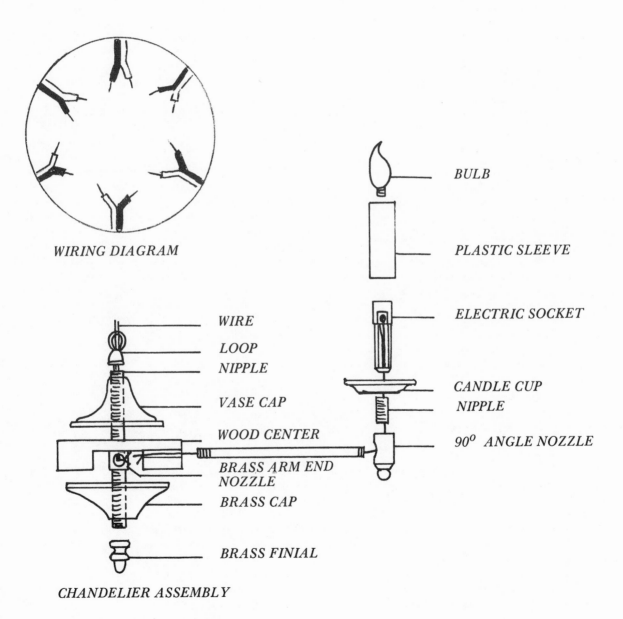

WIRING DIAGRAM

BULB

PLASTIC SLEEVE

ELECTRIC SOCKET

CANDLE CUP

NIPPLE

90° ANGLE NOZZLE

WIRE

LOOP

NIPPLE

VASE CAP

WOOD CENTER

BRASS ARM END
NOZZLE

BRASS CAP

BRASS FINIAL

CHANDELIER ASSEMBLY

EARLY AMERICAN
SIXTEEN ARM TIN CHANDELIER

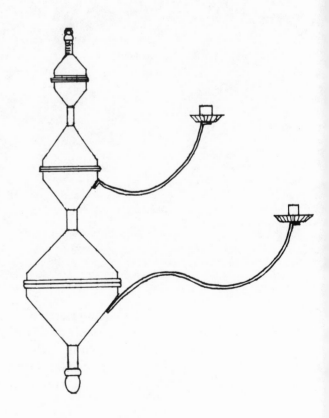

EARLY AMERICAN SIXTEEN ARM TIN
CHANDELIER

Here's a tin chandelier that re-creates the
simple, but elegant designs of early American
lighting. It's really quite easy to make, and will
grace your home with the beauty of candlelight
for years to come.

MATERIALS

2 Funnels 3" diameter
2 Funnels 4" diameter
2 Funnels 5" diameter
N. 18 Gauge sheet aluminum or tin
Tin snips or scissors
Rubber hammer
Rivet gun & rivets
Liquid solder -- 1 Tube

Electric drill
2 Pans 8" diameter & 7" diameter
23" Lamp pipe threaded both ends
1 Silver loop
Lamp chain
16 Aluminum molds
16 Candles
1 Wooden finial

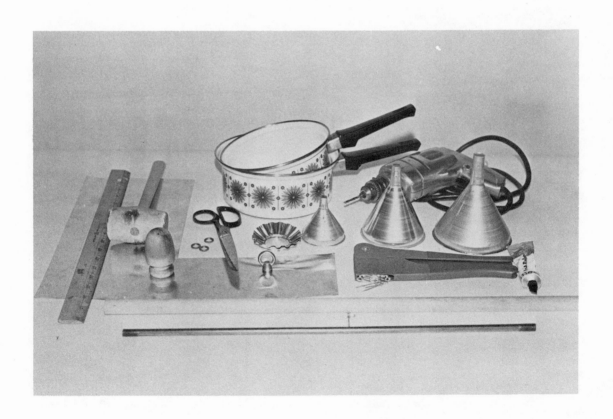

DIRECTIONS

STEP 2

STEP 1 -- Enlarge the diagram of the two chandelier arms. This will give you a guide to measure the arms.

STEP 2 -- With pencil and ruler, mark the arms on the sheet aluminum. Each arm is 1" wide with a 3/8" border on each side. Mark eight of these 15" long and eight 10½" long. With tin snips or scissors cut these out.

STEP 2

STEP 3

STEP 3 -- Place the arm under piece of wood as shown, leaving the 3/8" border out on the side. Two C-clamps will hold the wood and arm in place while you hammer the edge down. Take arm out from under the wood and finish hammering the edge down flat onto the arm. Follow the same procedure for the other edge of the arm. Do this for all of the arms. (See Photo)

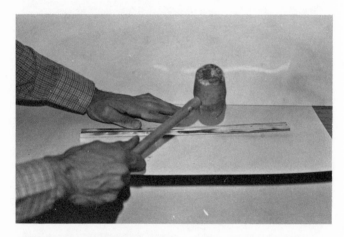

STEP 3

STEP 4 -- Using an 8" diameter pot as your form, slowly start hammering the 15" candle arm around the pot. Do not try to bend the arm completely the first time, but hammer it around the pot in stages. Use the guides you drew in Step 1 to help you in shaping each arm. Each arm needn't be a perfect match of the guide drawing, but a close approximation.

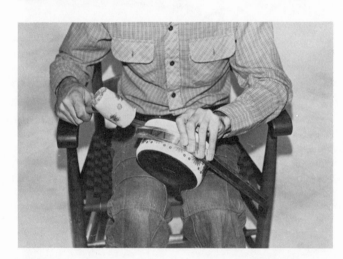

STEP 4

STEP 5 -- Use the 7" diameter pan to form the upper arms of the chandelier. Follow enlarged design as before. A 1" bend at each end of these arms will be required to affix the candle cups to the arms going to the funnel.

STEP 6 -- Drill hole in center of each candle cup, and drill holes into the ends of each arm following the diagram. Two holes in one end to affix each arm to funnel, and one hole in the other end to affix candle cups. (See Photo)

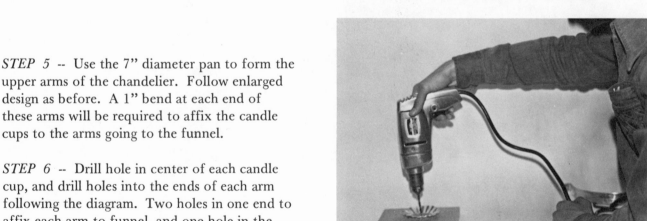

STEP 6

STEP 6

STEP 7

STEP 7 -- Place arm onto edge of funnel and with a pencil mark the placement of each hole. Then drill one hole into funnel. Now rivet arm to funnel. Make sure arm is straight and drill second hole into funnel using the second hole you previously drilled in the arms as a guide. Then rivet to funnel. Follow diagram to help in placement of the arms around funnel. Do this for the large 5" funnel and for the arms around the 4" funnel.

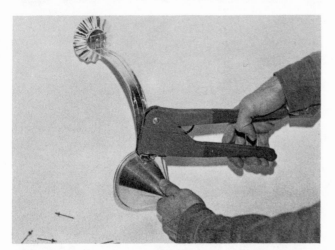

STEP 7

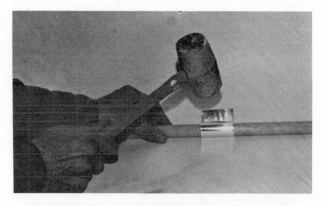

STEP 8

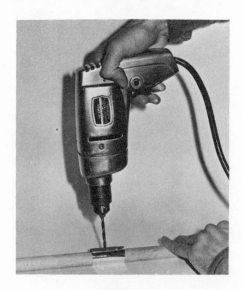

STEP 8 -- Follow diagram and cut 16 pieces 1½" x 3½" for the candle sleeves. Form these around a ¾" dowel stick or a broom handle. Overlap the ends ½" and drill a hole into both edges and rivet together.

STEP 8

STEP 8

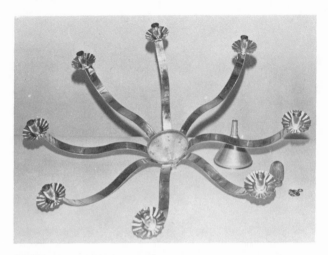

STEP 10

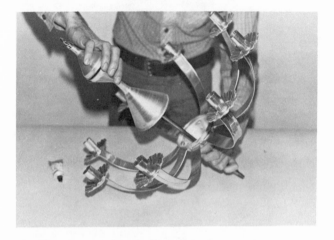

STEP 11

STEP 12

STEP 9 -- With liquid solder, solder each candle sleeve to the candle cups. Let dry for eight hours. If you place the funnel into a heavy bottle it will make it easier to solder the sleeves to the cup.

STEP 10 -- Rivet each candle cup to the arms of the chandelier.

STEP 11 -- Solder the funnels together with liquid solder.

STEP 12 -- Insert running thread pipe through the ends of the six funnels and secure at the top with a silver loop, and a ¾" bushing at the bottom.

STEP 13 -- Place wooden finial on end of funnel.

STEP 14 -- Insert chain into loop and hang.

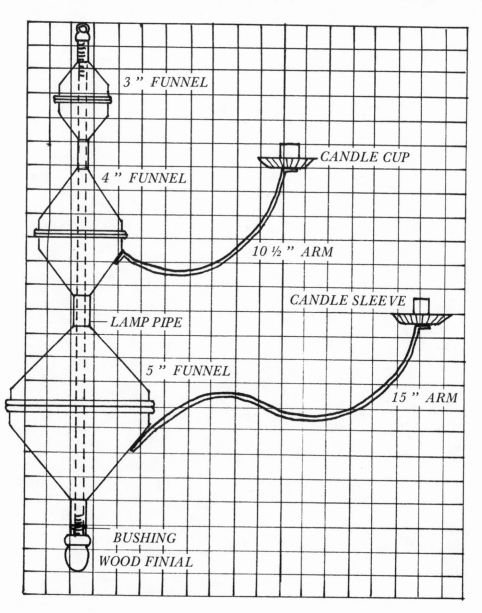

3 " FUNNEL

4 " FUNNEL

CANDLE CUP

10 ½ " ARM

LAMP PIPE

CANDLE SLEEVE

5 " FUNNEL

15 " ARM

BUSHING

WOOD FINIAL

EACH SQUARE 1 " SQ.

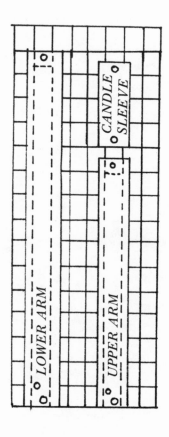

LOWER ARM

CANDLE SLEEVE

UPPER ARM

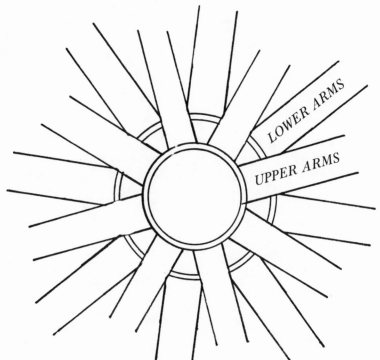

LOWER ARMS

UPPER ARMS

ARM PLACEMENT GUIDE

MORTISE MARKING GAUGE
CANDLE HOLDER

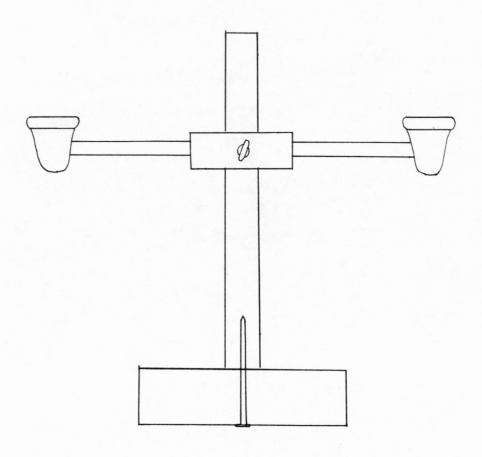

MORTISE MARKING GAUGE CANDLE
HOLDER

In this project, a carpenter's mortise
marking gauge was turned into a unique
adjustable candle holder.

MATERIALS

1 Wooden base 1" x 3" x 3½"
1 Nail
1 Mortise marking gauge
2 Wood candle cups
2 3" pieces of 3/8" brass tubing
Contact cement
Wood stain

DIRECTIONS

STEP 1 -- A mortise marking gauge forms the central part of the candle holder. These can be bought at a hardware, department, or lumber store.

STEP 2 -- Drill a 3/8" hole ½" in depth into the two sides of movable part of the marking gauge.

STEP 3 -- Drill a 3/8" hole ½" in depth into the sides of each wooden candle cup.

STEP 4 -- Cut piece of wood for base.

STEP 5 -- Cut two pieces of brass tubing 3 " long.

STEP 6 -- Nail marking gauge to base.

STEP 7 -- Adhere candle cups to tubing with contact cement. Then glue the other ends to the movable part of marking gauge.

STEP 8 -- With oil wood stain, paint all wood parts of candle holder.

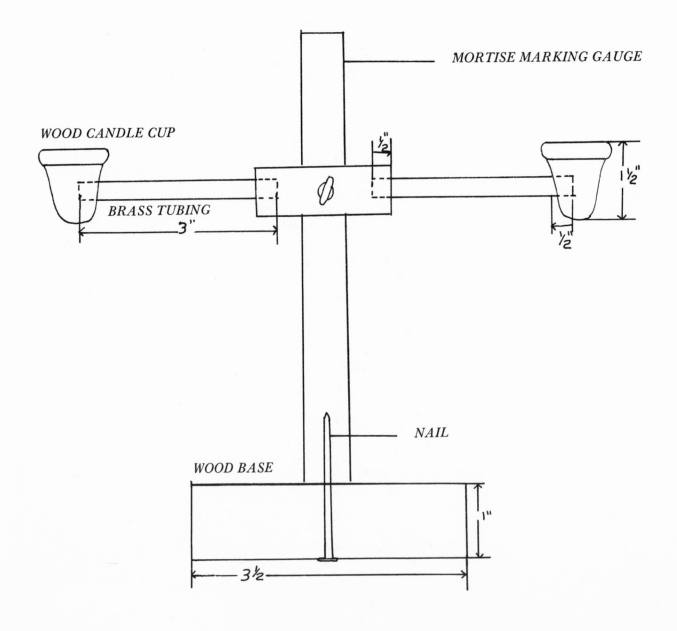

NEEDLEPOINT LAMP

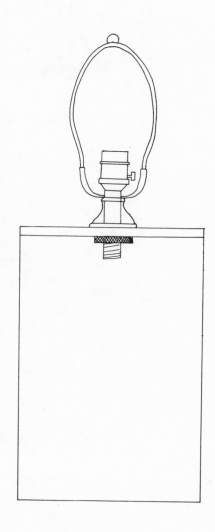

NEEDLEPOINT LAMP

Here's a lamp that will let you show off your
needlepoint skill as well as your lamp making
ability. This simple bargello stitch amkes an
interesting and beautiful base for your lamp.

DIRECTIONS

STEP 1 -- Cut pieces of plywood for lamp base. With nails and white glue, put base together.

STEP 2 -- With 3/8" drill bore hole into top center of base.

STEP 3 -- Follow pattern for bargello needle-point design, and complete the four sides. If you like, you can choose or design a needlepoint of your own choice.

STEP 4 -- Leave ½" of raw canvas on each side of design.. Stretch needlepoint canvas onto base, and staple to wood on raw canvas part.

STEP 5 -- Cut pieces of bamboo stripping and nail around edges of needlepoint.

STEP 6 -- Insert nipple into lamp base and adhere to base with locknut on bottom inside of base, and a threaded neck on the outside. Insert wire through nipple and connect to socket.

MATERIALS

½ " plywood 9" x 54"
11 ' of bamboo edging
1 Locknut
1 2" threaded nipple
1 Neck
1 Harp
1 Socket
1 8' parallel lamp cord
1 yd. of needlepoint canvas
Coats & Clarks' Persian-type needlepoint yarn
    (colors of your own choice)
Staple gun
1 Finial
1 Shade of your choice

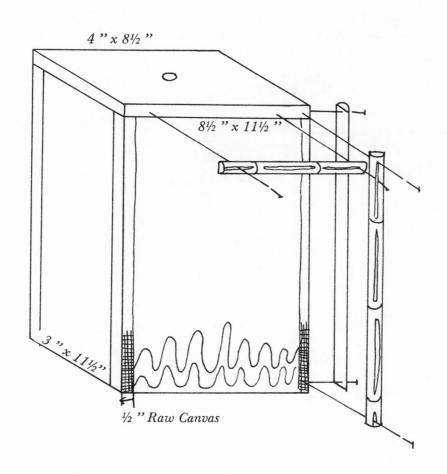

4 " x 8½ "

8½ " x 11½ "

3 " x 11½"

½ " Raw Canvas

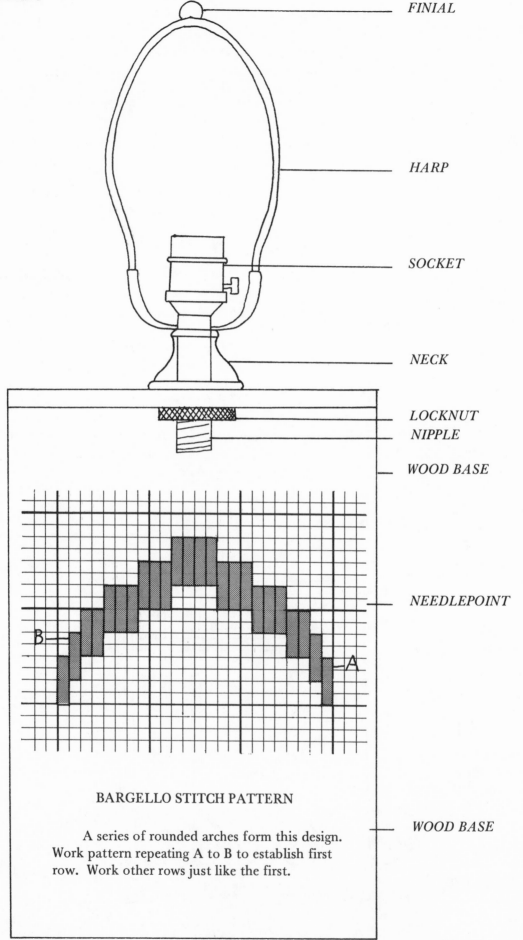

FINIAL

HARP

SOCKET

NECK

LOCKNUT

NIPPLE

WOOD BASE

NEEDLEPOINT

WOOD BASE

BARGELLO STITCH PATTERN

A series of rounded arches form this design.
Work pattern repeating A to B to establish first
row. Work other rows just like the first.

SOURCES

SUPPLIERS	SUPPLIES
Herter's Inc. Waseca, Minnesota 56093	Duck and snipe decoys, lamp kits, gourds; catalogue $1.
Lamp Specialties Co. 20 E. Willow Street Millburn, New Jersey 07041	Large selection of all types of lamp parts and lamp kits; excellent catalogue.
Albert Constantine & Son Inc. 2050 Eastchester Road Bronx, New York 10461 (212) SY 2 - 1600	Hardwoods, lamp parts; catalogue.
Minnesota Woodworkers Supply Co. Industrial Boulevard Rogers, Minnesota 55374 (612) 428 - 4101	Lamp parts; catalogue.
Grand Brass Lamp Parts 221 Grand Street New York, New York 10013 (212) CA 6 - 2567	Best place in New York for lamp supplies.
Lee Wards 1200 St. Charles Rd. Elgin, Illinois 60120	Lamp kits, yarns, canvas; free catalogue.
Nervo Studios 2027 7th Street Berkeley, California 94710	Lamp kits; catalogue $1.
Just Shades 188 Bowery New York, New York 10012	Complete selection of fine shades.
U. S. General Supply Corp. 100 General Place Jericho, New York 11753	Carborundum drill, rivet gun, wire stripper.

Bergen Arts & Crafts Inc.
Box 381
Marblehead, Massachusetts 01945

Lamp parts, lamps; catalogue $1.

San Francisco Stained Glass Works
3463 16th Street
San Francisco, California 94114

Tiffany style lamps, free price list.

Pewter by Lazor
371 West Mountain Road
West Simsbury, Connecticut 06092

Original pewter items, handcrafted. Tableware, jewelry and others. Catalogue and price list free.

Federal Smallwares
85 Fifth Avenue
New York, New York 10003

Doll reproductions, miniatures; catalogue.

Standard Dolls
23 - 83 31st St.,
Astoria, New York 11105

Doll reproductions, miniatures, doll parts; catalogue.

BIBLIOGRAPHY

Barber, Joel, *Wild Fowl Decoys,* New York:
    Dover Publications, 1970.

Burk, Bruce, *Game Bird Carving,* New York :
    Wichester Press, 1972.

Hebard, Helen Bringham, *Early Lighting in New England,*
    Vermont : Charles E. Tuttle Company, 1964.

Holbrook, Wallace W., *Contemporary Lamps,* Illinois:
    McKnight and McKnight Publishing Company, 1968.

Thwing, Leroy, *Flickering Flames,* Vermont :
    Charles E. Tuttle Company, 1959.